# INQUEST
# ON THE SHROUD
# OF TURIN

# INQUEST
# ON THE SHROUD
# OF TURIN

## by JOE NICKELL
### in collaboration with a panel of
### scientific & technical experts

*Prometheus Books*
Buffalo, New York 14215

Published 1983 by
Prometheus Books
700 East Amherst Street, Buffalo, NY 14215

Copyright 1983 by Joe Nickell

Library of Congress Catalog Card Number: 82-62457
ISBN: 0-87975-194-0

Printed in the United States of America

# Contents

# The Critical-Review Panel

MICHAEL M. BADEN, M.D., is deputy chief medical examiner of Suffolk County, New York. Formerly chief medical examiner of New York City, Dr. Baden is an associate professor of forensic medicine, New York University; visiting professor of pathology, Albert Einstein School of Medicine; lecturer in pathology, Columbia University College of Physicians and Surgeons; and adjunct professor of law, New York Law School.

JAMES R. BURKE, of James R. Burke Photographic Portraiture, Lexington, Kentucky, is a Photographic Craftsman and a Master of Photography, degrees conferred by Professional Photographers of America. He is also a member of the American Society of Photographers. He has lectured widely on the art of photographic portraiture.

JOHN F. FISCHER is a forensic analyst with the Orange County Sheriff's Office, Orlando, Florida. His fields of expertise include microchemical analyses (for example, those involving blood substances) and the development of organic and inorganic spot tests. He has testified in legal proceedings as to the chemical identity of bloodstains. He is the co-author of Chapter 12 and wrote the Appendix.

GERALD A. LARUE, professor of biblical history and archaeology at the University of Southern California, Los Angeles, serves as a technical consultant to the Committee for the Scientific Investigation of Claims of the Paranormal.

WAYNE MORRIS is a crime laboratory analyst with the Florida Department of Law Enforcement, Sanford Regional Crime Laboratory, Sanford, Florida. His expertise is chemical and instrumental analyses, with particular emphasis on molecular-structure determination by infrared spectroscopy.

5

MARVIN M. MUELLER, PH.D., is a research physicist in the laser fusion program at the Los Alamos National Laboratory in New Mexico. In addition to twenty years of work in diverse experimental and theoretical physics, he has experience in image analysis and a strong background in chemistry. He has recently published a new method for reconstructing three-dimensional sources from x-ray images. Dr. Mueller co-authored Chapter 8.

GLEN TAYLOR, a professional artist in Lexington, Kentucky, has fifteen years' experience in techniques ranging from pastel portraiture to bronze bas-relief sculpture. He has a strong background in art history and has done graduate work at the University of Kentucky in theatrical prosthetics (prefabricated facial appliances).

---

*Note: Affiliations are given for identification only and do not imply endorsement by an outside agency.*

# Preface

For six centuries the linen cloth now known as the "Shroud of Turin" has been the subject of controversy. To many, it is the Holy Shroud—the actual burial cloth of Christ. To others, Christians and agnostics among them, it is spurious, the product of a clever forger. Still others regard the "shroud" as an enigma—what one popular writer has termed "the World's Strangest Mystery."[1]

There have been other "true" shrouds, some with earlier (and to that extent, more convincing) historical records.[2] But the shroud of Turin is unique in at least one respect. Imprinted on its fourteen-foot length[3] are the front and back images of a bearded, apparently crucified man—strikingly similar to traditional depictions of Jesus, complete with "wounds" from the crown of thorns and the Roman soldier's lance.

Much of the controversy stems from this identification of the cloth as the Holy Shroud. As one early twentieth-century investigator, zoologist Yves Delage, stated when he was chastised by the French Academy for proclaiming the shroud genuine:

> A religious question has been needlessly injected into a problem which in itself is purely scientific, with the result that feelings have run high, and reason has been led astray. If, instead of Christ, there were a question of some person like a Sargon, an Achilles or one of the pharaohs, no one would have thought of making any objections.[4]

But Delage misstates the matter. Any such object would be suspect if—as is the case with the shroud— its whereabouts were unrecorded for thirteen centuries, and the earliest written record of it was a credible report claiming its forger had confessed. Moreover, no burial cloth in the history of the world is known to have borne such images of the body wrapped within it.

Nevertheless, from the turn of the century self-styled "sindonologists" (*sindon* is Greek for a linen cloth such as the shroud) have been crusading

7

for acceptance of the "relic" as authentic, although the Roman Catholic Church, which has tacit ownership, has never made such a claim. Advocacy for the "cause of the Holy Shroud"[5] has come from such sindonological groups as the International Center of Sindonology in Italy, the British Society for the Turin Shroud, and, in the United States, the Holy Shroud Guild, a Catholic organization of some four decades' standing. Two members of the Guild's Executive Council are also the leaders of the Shroud of Turin Research Project (STURP), a group of pro-authenticity scientists founded in 1977. The following year this group conducted an examination of the cloth.

At approximately the same time that STURP was being organized and making plans for its tests, I began my own investigation of the shroud. I was intrigued by the image's touted "photonegative" properties and the assertions that no artist could have produced such an image centuries before the invention of photography. I was also concerned about an obvious lack of objectivity on the part of most shroud investigators. Judging from their statements, it was apparent that they passionately believed the shroud genuine, even though they could not explain how the image was formed.

It seemed to me that solving the mystery of the image's formation could lead to an answer to the question of authenticity. This approach, I was convinced, was all the more important since Turin custodians were refusing to permit tests that could date the cloth.

After several months of research and experimentation, I was unable to explain the image in terms of natural (non-artistic) processes, and I saw no evidence to suggest a supernatural process. In any case, invoking a supernatural explanation would effectively end rational scientific inquiry, and would be justifiable only after all natural and artistic processes had been decisively eliminated. I therefore turned to artistry and finally succeeded in producing similar images by means of a medieval artistic process.

Following publication of my experimental results,[6] I was soon joined by John Fischer, a forensic analyst, and then by Dr. Marvin Mueller, a research physicist at the Los Alamos National Laboratory. Eventually our panel comprised several members (including Catholic, Protestant, Jew, and agnostic) with expertise in a wide range of scientific and technical fields applicable to the shroud investigation.

This book is a result of our collaborative efforts, although I should point out that (except where noted) authorship is mine, and I therefore assume responsibility for statements of fact and opinion. As a group, we continue to monitor the Shroud of Turin investigation closely, to advance hypotheses, and to test them experimentally whenever possible. I believe that this group meets an important need. Dr. Mueller has stated:

Science is done for diverse reasons. In common with most other human enter-prises, it is done by individuals having a great variety of motives, and unalloyed "truth for its own sake" is not always paramount. The main marvel of modern science is that useful, reliable, predictive knowledge *eventually* emerges from a chaos of contradictory opinions. These opinions are held by researchers who are all too obviously encumbered by common human frailties, such as fallibili-ty. For this reason, science in its self-corrective aspect needs, and thrives on, open, uninhibited airing of divergent opinions.[7]

In treating this multifaceted controversy, I have attempted to avoid un-necessary technicality; however, given the nature of many of the tests and hypotheses, some of the discussions are necessarily technical. And so we must distinguish between the shroud's microscopic properties and its macroscopic ones (that is, those visible to the naked eye), between threads and fibers (which make up individual threads), and so forth. But if we often focus on the microscopic and other technical aspects, we will endeavor not to lose sight of, so to speak, the larger picture.

The Spanish philosopher Ortega y Gasset wrote, "The minimum is the measuring unit in the realm of quantity, but in the realm of values, the highest values are the measuring unit."[8] Among those values must surely be a desire to *attempt* to learn the truth; that has prompted this study.

# 1

# The Scandal at Lirey

Sometime in the middle of the fourteenth century the cloth now known as the "Shroud of Turin" made its first recorded appearance in Lirey, a small provincial town in the diocese of Troyes, in north-central France. Troyes lies a short distance southeast of Paris.

Some authorities give the date as 1353,[1] at which time they believe Geoffroy de Charny, known as the "perfect knight," presented the "shroud" to the Dean of the proposed Lirey abbey. This is by no means certain, for although the church was established in June of 1353 by Geoffroy himself, who obtained a "rent" from King Jean II (called John the Good)[2], there is no documentary evidence to support the claim that it was specifically founded to enshrine the cloth.[3] But we do know that relics frequently served as the impetus for the building of a church.

In any case, the wooden collegiate church, named Our Lady of Lirey and dedicated to the Annunciation in 1353, was completed in 1356 and officially inaugurated on May 28.[4] In 1357 (the year after the death of Geoffroy, killed September 19, 1356, during the Battle of Poitiers) a list of the relics of the abbey was recorded. The shroud was not mentioned.[5] But, argued Paul Vignon, an early twentieth-century shroud advocate, it is important to note "that in 1355 the Charny family resumed the charge of the sacred relic, and that it remained in their keeping until 1389."[6]

We do know that by about 1357 the shroud was placed on view by the canons of Lirey. Great crowds of pilgrims thronged to exhibitions of the "relic," which was shown at full length and advertised as the "true Burial Sheet of Christ."[7] Medallions were struck in commemoration of this event. Presumably these were sold as somewhat expensive souvenirs. One of these medallions survived and was discovered by a Frenchman named A. Forgeais in 1855. Forgeais, who made a business of dredging up treasures from the

11

Seine, found the shroud medallion embedded in mud by the Pont au Change, and today it is in the collection of the Musée de Cluny in Paris.

The embossed medallion image shows the full-length shroud with its ventral and dorsal images in bold relief. This is one of several indications that the imagery was formerly much stronger than the faint sepia images of today, some six centuries later. Two cope-attired churchmen hold the cloth stretched between them. A roundel at the lower center of the medallion, just below the shroud, depicts the empty sepulcher of the risen Christ, and flanking either side of the roundel are two shields: on the left the coat of arms of Geoffroy de Charny, and on the right the arms of his second wife, Jeanne de Vergy.[8] This pilgrim's medallion is the earliest known authentic record of the shroud. Before this are thirteen centuries of silence.

This silence—this complete lack of provenance for the purported relic— was one of several reasons the shroud's authenticity was questioned at the time it was first exhibited. Another was the fact that New Testament writers failed to mention the imprint of Jesus' body on his shroud. For such reasons, the bishop of Troyes, Henri de Poitiers, at the urging of "many theologians and other wise persons" launched an investigation.

We know of this first investigation from a lengthy report sent to the Pope in 1389 by a successor to Henri, Bishop Pierre d'Arcis. The d'Arcis memorandum[9] is a powerful charge against the authenticity of the shroud. D'Arcis begins:

> The case, Holy Father, stands thus. Some time since in this diocese of Troyes the Dean of a certain collegiate church, to wit, that of Lirey, falsely and deceitfully, being consumed with the passion of avarice, and not from any motive of devotion but only of gain, procured for his church a certain cloth cunningly painted, upon which by a clever sleight of hand was depicted the twofold image of one man, that is to say, the back and front, he falsely declaring and pretending that this was the actual shroud in which our Saviour Jesus Christ was enfolded in the tomb.

D'Arcis continues:

> This story was put about not only in the kingdom of France, but, so to speak, throughout the world, so that from all parts people came together to view it. And further to attract the multitude so that money might cunningly be wrung from them, pretended miracles were worked, certain men being hired to represent themselves as healed at the moment of the exhibition of the shroud, which all believed to be the shroud of our Lord.

The Bishop of Troyes, says his successor, had become aware of these deceptive practices and was "urged by many prudent persons to take action, as indeed was his duty in the exercise of his ordinary jurisdiction."

It is significant that not only had the Bishop's permission for the exhibition *not* been sought, but also that he had been circumvented in the founding of the Lirey church.[10] While he eventually gave his approval, it was not until nearly three years later, when he spoke at the inauguration of the completed abbey and praised Geoffroy de Charny.

Why had the Bishop been bypassed? A possible answer suggests itself if we accept Paul Vignon's claim (p. 11) that the shroud was in Geoffroy's possession in 1353 and if we adopt the reasonable but unverifiable hypothesis that the church was built to house the shroud. In brief, the Bishop of Troyes may have been circumvented because he had expressed skepticism about the shroud's authenticity and had refused to condone the building of a church for the purpose of venerating it. Geoffroy may in turn have decided to withdraw the shroud, thus obtaining the Bishop's subsequent approval for the church.

What we do know is that when the shroud was exhibited—whether before 1357 by Geoffroy or in 1357 by his widow—the Bishop did conduct an investigation, the result of which was reportedly the discovery of the forger who created the shroud and confessed. In d'Arcis' words:

> Eventually, after diligent inquiry and examination, he discovered the fraud and how the said cloth had been cunningly painted, *the truth being attested by the artist who had painted it,* to wit, that it was a work of human skill and not miraculously wrought or bestowed. [Italics added for emphasis.]

As a result, the Bishop took action:

> Accordingly, after taking mature counsel with wise theologians and men of the law, seeing that he neither ought nor could allow the matter to pass, he began to institute formal proceedings against the said Dean and his accomplices in order to root out this false persuasion. They, seeing their wickedness discovered, hid away the said cloth so that the Ordinary could not find it, and they kept it hidden afterwards for thirty-four years or thereabouts down to the present year.

Subtracting d'Arcis' thirty-four years from "the present year" (1389) would place the time of the first exhibition and resulting investigation in 1355—"or thereabouts."

In 1389 the shroud was brought out of its hiding place (rumored to have been outside the diocese[11]) and was exhibited once again. And once again the bishop of the diocese, Pierre d'Arcis, was circumvented. In this instance we have a clearer indication of why the Bishop was bypassed: D'Arcis knew the results of the earlier investigation and, as a man of integrity and conscience, would have forbidden exhibition of what he believed, on the evidence, to be a spurious relic.

Therefore the Dean of the Lirey church and its patron, the second Geoffroy de Charny, embarked upon a two-pronged course of action. First, bypassing d'Arcis, they sought official permission by going over his head. They applied to the cardinal legate, Peter of Thury, who happened to be in the area at the time. As we shall see, they seem to have misrepresented the truth, thereby deceiving the Cardinal, who, "without entirely approving the petition," reports d'Arcis, allowed exhibition of the shroud.

The second part of the plan was to downplay the claim made at the earlier exhibition that the shroud was the authentic shroud of Christ. Nevertheless, the Dean and "his accomplices" (to use the Bishop's term), including five canons of the church plus Geoffroy, avoided advertising the cloth frankly as an artist's production. Instead they made public announcements, in which they played games with semantics, and also circulated false rumors. According to d'Arcis:

> Although it is not publicly stated to be the true shroud of Christ, nevertheless this is given out and noised abroad in private, and so it is believed by many, the more so, because, as stated above, it was on the previous occasion declared to be the true shroud of Christ, and by a certain ingenious manner of speech it is now in the said church styled not the *sudarium* [a burial cloth] but the *sanctuarium* [that is, "relic"], which to the ears of the common folk, who are not keen to observe distinctions, sounds much the same thing.

Here d'Arcis shows himself a man of conscience; for, rather than maintain a comfortable silence and wash his hands of the matter, he decided to take action that he knew might provoke the ire of the Cardinal and others. He ordered that the exhibition cease and threatened the Dean with excommunication if he persisted.

The Dean did however persist; he even launched an appeal. Not only that, but Geoffroy obtained from King Charles VI of France (again, as we shall see, apparently under false pretenses) a royal warrant (*salvagordia*) and even a royal military honor guard to attend the exhibition. There the shroud was displayed upon a high platform flanked with flaming torches. And "the knight" — Geoffroy de Charny — even publicly venerated the cloth by holding it in his own hands on at least one feast occasion.[12]

D'Arcis, although he felt rather "powerless," nevertheless continued to launch prohibitions and sentences of excommunication against those who exhibited the cloth. He felt that his actions were "in no wise derogatory to the said Lord Cardinal's letters," since these had been obtained "surreptitiously" and "by no means conceded that the cloth could be exposed with publicity or venerated," but only that it might be given a place of safekeeping.

Bishop d'Arcis now turned to the King, who heard the full details for the first time. D'Arcis won a minor victory: the King ordered that the cloth be surrendered and, to insure that this was carried out, he instructed the Bailiff of Troyes to seize it. While we see from the King's actions confirmation that the custodians of the shroud had deceived him with half-truths, even his royal order was not to prevail. The Bailiff of Troyes returned from his trip carrying not the cloth of Lirey but merely word of the Dean's emphatic refusal. Still extant is his report of 1389 stating that the shroud was a painting.[13]

Eventually Geoffroy applied secretly to Clement VII, the Avignon pope (the first of the antipopes in the Great Western Schism),[14] with the result that, without investigating the matter or hearing d'Arcis, Clement imposed silence on the Bishop. Why Clement would behave in favor of Geoffroy is puzzling until we consider that Geoffroy was a close relation of Clement. His mother, the widow Jeanne de Vergy, had shrewdly remarried; her second husband was Clement's wealthy uncle. She may have thought, suggests shroud historian Ian Wilson, that "such a matrimonial alliance would both seal old wounds and provide her son with useful connections to what was a highly episcopal family."[15] In another move, which would potentially salve old wounds, Geoffroy had married Marguerite de Poitiers, niece of Bishop Henri de Poitiers.

Pierre d'Arcis was an outsider. Still, despite further risks to himself, he refused to remain silent. In late 1389 he sat down and drafted his lengthy memorandum to Pope Clement VII. He recounted the basic facts of the earlier investigation and defended himself against the false accusations of the shroud promoters who, he says, accused him of jealousy and even of desiring to possess the shroud himself—apparently for purposes of exploiting it for his own gain, although d'Arcis' outspoken condemnations of the shroud in effect guaranteed that he could never have profited from it, even had he wanted to.

D'Arcis backed his evidence and defense with an implicit challenge to the Lirey hawkers: "I offer myself here," he wrote, "as ready to supply all information sufficient to remove any doubt concerning the facts alleged both from public report and otherwise." No doubt there were among d'Arcis' "many prudent advisers" (some of whom averred that he moved "too half-heartedly in the matter" and made himself "a laughing-stock by allowing the abuse to continue")[16] persons still living who knew the facts of the first investigation.

If it were d'Arcis, and not the shroud's owners, who were acting deceitfully, the latter had a ready opportunity to prove their case by the simple expediency of *explaining how the "shroud" came into their possession.* But instead they maintained silence.

The first Geoffroy de Charny had never explained how he, a man of modest means, had acquired what would have been, *if* it were authentic, the most fabulous relic in all of Christendom.[17] Even many present-day defenders of the shroud's authenticity concede that Geoffroy's silence implies some guilty secret, but they prefer to fantasize that it involved Geoffroy's acquisition of the shroud (possibly by some illegal means)[18] rather than that its provenance led directly to the studio of an artist who had confessed it was his handiwork. Ian Wilson, for example, concedes:

> ...the de Charnys' guilt seemed to be independently demonstrated by various factors, not least of which is that they failed to make any attempt to explain how they acquired the cloth. If the shroud was genuine, such an explanation would surely have put an end to the matter.[19]

Geoffroy's survivors and descendants—his wife, his son, and later his granddaughter Margaret—all exhibited the shroud and profited from it. Either they did not know how Geoffroy had obtained the cloth or chose, for reasons which remain unclear, to offer vague, unconvincing, and conflicting stories about its acquisition. Son Geoffroy asserted it was a "gift," whereas Margaret alleged it was a *butin de guerre* (a spoil of war).[20] Geoffroy's widow, Jeanne de Vergy, like her husband, said nothing at all.

Since the Charny family failed to respond to d'Arcis' implicit challenge, their silence would seem to be further evidence (in addition to that already given, with more yet to follow) that d'Arcis knew the true facts; given the opportunity to augment the basic facts (necessarily summarized in what he regarded as a preliminary memorandum), the Bishop could prove the truth about the "shroud" revealed in two investigations. As he stated, he could not "fully or sufficiently express in writing the grievous nature of the scandal."

Hence, Bishop d'Arcis made an impassioned plea to Clement. He expressed his fear of the "danger to souls." He summarized the facts concerning "the delusion and scandal" resulting from the cloth's exhibition and warned of "the contempt brought upon the Church and ecclesiastical jurisdiction." And he insisted on fulfilling his duty under canon law "to see that no man be imposed upon by false representations and documents for the purpose of gain."

Clement—while still allowing exhibition of the cloth and again enjoining d'Arcis to perpetual silence on the matter—made an important determination of the shroud's authenticity based on the evidence before him. Whether he obtained further evidence (beyond d'Arcis' letter) or inquired privately among other knowledgeable persons, we do not know. At least he had before him the evidence of investigations conducted by two bishops whose veracity he knew. Against this was the silence of the Charny family and the dean and canons of the Lirey abbey. If Clement consulted his advisors and other theologians, they no doubt pointed out the commonsense reasons for skepticism that had prompted Henri de Poitiers to launch the first investigation: namely, that the gospels make no mention of an imaged shroud (a fact the evangelists surely would not have omitted had it been true) and that it was unlikely such a fact "should have remained hidden until the present time."

Therefore, with overwhelming evidence against authenticity—complete, it seemed, with the forger's confession—and no evidence in favor, Clement decided that the cloth of Lirey was merely that, a painted cloth and not a shroud. While public exhibitions could continue (a concession to his Charny kin), severe restrictions were placed on the exhibitions. First, Clement decreed, all ceremonies must be omitted. There were to be no candles nor incense nor guard of honor. Second, he ordered that whenever the cloth was exhibited it be loudly announced each time that "it is not the True Shroud of Our Lord, but a painting or picture made in the semblance or representation of the shroud."[21]

On January 6, 1390, Clement affixed his signature to the documents that collectively settled the matter. In addition to a letter each to Geoffroy and Bishop d'Arcis, he wrote to various other church authorities in the diocese (specifically the ecclesiastical judges of Autun, Langres, and Châlons-sur-Marne) instructing them to see that his restrictions were adhered to.[22] Thus ended the first long and scandalous episode in the history of the shroud. Pierre d'Arcis died in 1395 and Geoffroy followed three years later.

But soon there would be another series of scandals involving the cloth, and at the center would be still another generation of Charnys. For Margaret de Charny was as obstinate as her father and grandfather. Through her actions Margaret prepared the way for the cloth eventually to become—more than a century after her death—the shroud of Turin.

In 1400, two years after her father's death, the young Margaret married Jean de Baufremont, who was killed in the Battle of Agincourt in 1415. Margaret was soon again at the altar, marrying a wealthy count named Humbert de Villersexel.

When war threatened Lirey and hence her grandfather's church and the "representation" of the shroud it contained, Margaret and Humbert obtained permission from the Lirey canons to house the cloth for safety in the Charny castle, Montfort, located near Montbard. Humbert issued in his own hand a receipt dated July 6, 1418, which covered various "jewels and relics," including the cloth. He fully acknowledged it to be a painted fake when he described it as "a cloth, on which is the figure or representation of the Shroud of Our Lord Jesus Christ, which is in a casket emblazoned with the de Charny crest."[23]

Humbert's receipt explicitly promised that when the present hostilities ended (the Hundred Years' War was still devastating France), the jewels and all relics—including the cloth—would be returned to the abbey. Instead, however, it was soon transferred to a chapel at St. Hippolyte sur Doubs, the seat of Humbert's domain as Count de la Roche. There, through Humbert's death in 1438, until 1453, the cloth remained in Margaret's possession. In 1443 the canons of Lirey served notice on Margaret, insisting that she return the cloth as promised. She observed that it was her husband, not she, who had signed the receipt and that she was not bound by the signature of her dead spouse.[24]

On May 9, 1443, the parliment of Dôle summoned Margaret and ordered that she return all the jewels and relics to Lirey; she was allowed to retain the cloth for three years in return for payments made toward the upkeep of the Lirey abbey. Apparently the canons missed the revenues from donations by generous pilgrims while the cloth was in their possession.

During these years, there were annual exhibitions of the cloth in a meadow near St. Hippolyte sur Doubs. Judging from Wilson's statement that "a minicult of the Shroud appears to have grown up, with many copies made,"[25] it seems likely that Margaret was following the Charny family tradition of falsely claiming—or at least suggesting—that an artist's rendering was actually Christ's shroud.

Margaret proved, in any case, that her word was meaningless, for again she failed to return the cloth to Lirey as she had been ordered and as she had agreed. She was summoned before the court of Besançon. But Margaret managed to stall successfully and was able to extend her possession for two more years and then for an additional three—each time by agreeing to pay the Lirey canons' court costs plus additional payments for church upkeep, all the while tendering her promise to return the monetarily valuable cloth. Not only did Margaret break her promises to return the cloth but she also failed to meet her obligation to pay compensation to the canons of Lirey.[26]

Instead she took the cloth on tour, holding exhibitions in the diocese of Liège in Belgium. In Chimay, in 1449, the rumor went far and wide that the "shroud" was authentic; while we cannot say that Margaret was directly responsible for the rumors, we can be certain that she did not clearly proclaim the cloth to be only an artist's "representation." Our certainty comes from the fact that had she done so there would not have been a need for a bishop's investigation of the purported relic's authenticity—the third in the cloth's history.

The Bishop of Liège, Jean de Heinsberg, was suspicious of the claims for authenticity. He therefore appointed a team of two theology professors to investigate the matter. As part of their investigation, they required Margaret to give evidence as to the shroud's provenance; all she could do was claim that it was a "spoil of war" and produce the documents allowing her to exhibit the "representation." Each of the four documents Margaret produced (according to a contemporary chronicler named Zantifliet) made clear that the cloth was *not* authentic.[27] The chronicler noted that the image on the cloth was "admirably depicted" and seemed to have been produced by some "astonishing art."[28]

Margaret returned south. In 1452 she showed it publicly at Germolles Castle, near Mâcon. There may have been another investigation like that at Chimay, for as Wilson states, this exhibition "seems to have been similarly abortive."[29]

The following year found Margaret in Geneva, where she appeared at the court of the House of Savoy. There she was a party to what Wilson terms "a curious transaction." Expressed simply, Margaret sold the cloth to Duke Louis I of Savoy and received in return the castle of Varambon and the fief (manor house and town) of Mirabel, near Lyon. (Wilson says that Margaret was to receive the *revenues* of Mirabel; Humber states that when Mirabel had "been taken from her" [Sox explains that the revenues "were already exhausted"] she received as compensation the estate of Flumet in 1455.)[30]

Some shroud writers, generally pro-authenticity ones who portray Margaret in the best possible light, say that Margaret "gave" the cloth to Duke Louis and that in return the Duke "gave" her the property. Actually the "curious transaction" was not so curious. In return for "valuable service" (that is, transferring ownership of the cloth to the Savoys) Margaret was paid handsomely. A century later Margaret's supposed generosity had been colorfully embroidered into an apocryphal tale that related how the pious woman rode astride a mule carrying the shroud to Burgundy. Outside the gate of Chambery the prescient beast came to a halt and stubbornly refused to go any farther. Margaret, knowing of the Duke's wife's desire to possess the relic, saw this as a sign, which she humbly heeded.[31]

Actually, at this time, the pious woman of later legend was on the sure road toward excommunication. By 1457 events had reached a crisis. The canons of Lirey, possibly aware by now of Margaret's sale of the cloth (however much the fact had been shrewdly camouflaged as "valuable service" in an obscure document in another region), had neared the end of their patience. After a pro forma warning to her to return the shroud to its owners, the ecclesiastical judge of Besançon finally, on May 30, 1457,[32] issued a formal writ of excommunication against Margaret.

Margaret responded with her usual entreaties. This time she promised to compensate the Lirey canons for the loss of their shroud. The sum was to be 800 gold ducats. Margaret paid neither a ducat nor a copper to Lirey, and so, on January 19, 1458, she was summoned by the provost of Troyes.

As in 1449 when she had previously been summoned before the provost, Margaret was represented in absentia by her half-brother, Charles de Noyers. This time Charles lent his own name to the usual promises, guaranteeing the 800-ducat sum plus an additional 300 pounds to reimburse the Lirey canons for their court costs. Charles also promised to surrender the cloth's documents (primarily the papal bulls) that proved the canons' ownership of the cloth. In return it was agreed that Margaret's sentence of excommunication would be suspended in the interim and lifted completely if and when payment was made by October 1, 1458.[33] By this time, it seems, the Lirey canons were all but reconciled to the loss of the cloth and now hoped merely for compensation.

Margaret did nothing toward fulfilling the obligations pledged on her behalf; and two years later, on October 7, 1460,[34] she died. Having been childless, she was the last of the Charny line. In subsequent years the canons of Lirey would frequently have occasion to speak of Margaret, "upon whose memory," writes Thomas Humber, "they heaped reproofs, and from whose agent, Philibert Thibaut, they refused to lift the ban of excommunication."[35]

The Lirey affair continued briefly after Margaret's death as the canons sought to obtain their valuable cloth from the House of Savoy. But they fared scarcely better than they had with Margaret. Writing from Paris on February 6, 1461, Duke Louis mentioned vaguely how Margaret had "transferred" the cloth to the Savoys. Louis assigned to the canons an annual income of fifty gold franks in compensation for the loss of the revenues the cloth had brought the abbey.

In 1472[36] the Lirey canons petitioned the king of France to intervene in an attempt to collect the revenues, which had gone unpaid at Louis' death. They also sent representatives to a Savoy regent to claim arrears in the promised revenue. We do not know if these petitions were successful, but there was now no doubt that the cloth was irretrievably lost to the canons. Deprived of the monies which once, stated d'Arcis, "might cunningly be wrung" from pilgrims, the wooden church fell into neglect. Some have suggested it was because of the deteriorating condition of the abbey that Margaret sought to find the shroud a new home; but it seems more likely that it was the loss of revenues precipitated by Margaret's actions that caused the church to fall into disrepair. Even if Margaret believed the shroud authentic—which is doubtful in the extreme—she could have acted in a far different, certainly more honorable, manner had she been motivated by piety rather than financial considerations.

We would know little if anything about the scandals at Lirey were it not for the painstaking efforts of a scholarly French priest, Cyr Ulysse Chevalier, a medievalist. Recipient of the Legion of Honor at the age of 36, he became renowned for his monumental work, *Repetoire des Sources historiques du moyen age,* an annotated sourcebook on the history of the Middle Ages, which he wrote between 1875 and 1883.

One commentator termed him "the most learned man in France and perhaps in the entire world," and John Walsh, in his own discussion of the "peculiar affair at Lirey," writes:

> Chevalier possessed, to an extreme degree, some of the rarer abilities of the historian. He seemed, for instance, to have an affinity for old documents, an instinct for finding original records that had lain undisturbed for centuries in the dusky darkness of archives, libraries and collections. His competence in deciphering the strange, cramped handwriting of dead ages was almost unique. In handling his sources, he possessed a truly impressive ability to digest mountains of material; for one of his studies, a history of the Dauphine, he had carefully worked his way through more than 20,000 original documents.[37]

Canon Chevalier set himself to the task of uncovering the true history of the so-called shroud of Turin. When he completed his work he had uncovered fifty documents: among them were Pierre d'Arcis' valuable memorandum to Pope Clement VII, the report of 1389 by the Bailiff of Troyes, the decrees of Clement, and numerous other documents by which we have learned what we have about the "grievous nature of the scandal" (in d'Arcis' words) at Lirey. In 1900, Chevalier published at Paris his *Etude critique sur l'origine du Saint Suaire de Lirey-Chambéry-Turin* (Critical Study on the Origin of the Holy Shroud of Lirey-Chambéry-Turin). His exposé of the false relic earned him a gold medal; and, says Humber, "most reputable scholars wrote the shroud off as one of the more bizarre curiosities of church history and went on to more serious endeavors."[38]

Chevalier's amassed evidence is impressive. From it we learn that Bishop Henri de Poitiers and others were suspicious of the fact that no imaged shroud was mentioned in the gospels, and that the touted relic was utterly lacking in provenance—suspicions which remain strong arguments against authenticity. From Chevalier we know—what some shroud propagandists seem to wish we did not—that there were several investigations of the cloth of Lirey and that the first of these reportedly uncovered the artist who confessed to having created it. We know from Chevalier's documents that the owners of the shroud were unable to say how they had acquired it, that they hid it away after the first investigation, that they behaved in an underhanded fashion in attempting to exhibit the cloth as genuine, and that they even staged fake cures in the course of their profiting from its exhibition. And we know of Margaret de Charny's empty promises and failure to obey judicial authority, which resulted in her excommunication. Chevalier himself concluded: "The history of the shroud constitutes a protracted violation of the two virtues so often commended by our holy books, justice and truth."[39]

# 2

# From Chambéry to Turin

At the death of Margaret de Charny, the cloth of Lirey was firmly in the possession of the House of Savoy, a dynasty founded in 1003 that ruled Savoy and the Piedmont (extending from southeastern France across the Alps to northwestern Italy) for some nine centuries and, after 1860, the Kingdom of Italy. The founder of the dynasty was a feudal lord known as Umberto the White-handed; it is a later Umberto, the deposed monarch of Italy, who today owns the Savoy family heirloom called the shroud of Turin.

The fifteen-century Savoy who bought the cloth from Margaret, Duke Louis I, was the son of Amadeus VIII of Savoy. Although not a priest, Amadeus had been elected the schismatic pope, Felix V, who served for a decade before his abdication in 1449.

An earlier ancestor of Louis had been the king of France, Louis IX (known as St. Louis), who had once acquired the putative Holy Crown of Thorns for Sainte Chapelle in Paris.[1] Louis may have felt he was following family tradition in thus purchasing the cloth of Lirey; but it may have been that his wife was the motivating force, since Louis is described as "indolent, incapable, and ruled by his wife."[2]

Louis' domineering wife was Anne of Lusignan, daughter of the King of Cyprus, whose ancestors had reigned in Jerusalem during the Crusades. The Lusignan monarchs still affected the meaningless title, "King of Jerusalem," and Louis acquired the title after an otherwise unrewarding expedition to Cyprus at the urging of his wife.

As we have seen, Louis and Anne bought the shroud from Margaret in 1453. According to tradition, Anne had wished to acquire it earlier. Several factors may have come together to make 1453 an opportune time for Margaret to "give" Anne the cloth. The aging Margaret may have tired of confrontations with suspicious churchmen like those at Chimay and, possibly, Germolles. Then too, there were her legal problems with the persistent canons of Lirey. Lacking title to the cloth—indeed accused of illegally possessing it, a charge she was unable to defend herself against—Margaret may have found it difficult to sell the "relic."

Even the wealthy Louis and the determined Anne may have found it difficult to purchase the cloth, particularly since Louis' father was an antipope from 1439-1449 and lived until 1451. Before becoming Pope Felix V, he had established a uniform statute of laws for his entire duchy, despite the opposition of the wealthy families and cities who found their privileges thus curtailed. Felix may have been opposed to any suggestion that a relic officially branded as spurious be purchased and exhibited as genuine. As an Avignon pope, he would have had little difficulty in learning the truth of the scandal at Lirey by simply consulting the earlier antipope's—Clement's—decrees on the affair.

Whatever the actual facts of the matter, it was not long after Louis' father died that the reigning couple made the purchase. Interestingly, the year was the hundredth anniversary of the founding of the Lirey abbey, where the cloth had first appeared.

As soon as they acquired the cloth of Lirey—whether or not with the documents that stated it was merely an artist's rendering—the Savoys exhibited it as the true shroud. One imagines it attracted considerable revenues then as it certainly did afterward.

Writing a decade later, in 1464, the theologian Francesco della Rovere referred to "the Shroud in which the body of Christ was wrapped," which he said was "preserved with great devotion by the Dukes of Savoy."[3] From its reported creation in an artist's studio, through long years of controversy and scandal to the glittering court of the Savoys, now—at Louis' death in 1465—the cloth of Lirey was widely accepted as the Holy Shroud of Christ. It seems this designation would not be seriously challenged again until the beginning of the twentieth century.

Moreover, the Savoys were now claiming the "shroud" had magical protective powers, divinely bestowed of course, to be invoked in troubling times. According to Ian Wilson: "In the earliest days with the family it was carried about with them on their travels like a holy charm, to safeguard them against the dangers of a journey."[4] (This regard of the shroud as a "palladium"—St. Francis de Sales' term for it—persisted into later ages, as we shall see.) For example, the shroud was taken to Vercelli, where, on Good Friday, 1494, it was exhibited by Bianca, Duchess of Savoy.[5] Another journey may have taken the shroud as far as Lierre, Belgium. There in the archives of the St. Gommare Church is an artist's copy, dated 1516.[6]

Subsequently a new home was prepared for the shroud. After Amadeus IX of Savoy succeeded his father, Louis, he applied to Pope Sixtus IV to authorize the creation of a sanctuary for the shroud. In 1471 Sixtus gave his authorization, along with a number of privileges granted the church clergy. Amadeus then began to enlarge the ducal church and to embellish it in a manner suitable for the exhibition of such a great "relic."

On June 11, 1502, the new edifice was completed, and with great fanfare the cloth was lodged in its new home. Bearing the cross and lights, a procession of all the richly vestured clergy of Chambéry—with the Bishop of Grenoble carrying the shroud—made its way through the streets to the high altar of the chapel. There it was briefly exhibited, and then placed in a recess behind the altar which was secured by iron doors "and locked by four keys."[7]

In 1506 the chapel was formally given the appellation, the Sainte Chapelle of the Holy Shroud. This transpired as the result of a petition to Pope Julius II, who also instituted a special Feast of the Holy Shroud to be celebrated with its own Mass and Office on May 4. Pope Leo X extended the feast to all of Savoy, and Pope Gregory XIII extended it further to Piedmont.[8]

With such official sanction, celebrations, and attendant publicity, the Sainte Chapelle of the Holy Shroud attracted countless pilgrims—notable among them Queen Anne of Brittany in 1511 and, in 1515, the king of France, Francis I. It consequently attracted great revenues and treasures in the form of gifts, including "stained glass, Flemish sculpture, rich draperies, ornamentation from Cyprus, jewel-studded reliquaries." (The shroud received a new reliquary in 1509, the gift of Margaret of Austria.)[9]

But for all the good fortune (literally through revenues) which the shroud brought, its reputed palladian powers were soon to be sorely challenged—by fire and war. Yet the shroud itself would need to be protected; that protection would come from Savoy subjects, whose only talismans seemed to be a sincere piety and genuine courage.

On December 4, 1532—a fateful date in the shroud's history—a fire swept through the Sainte Chapelle of the Holy Shroud and flames licked at the silver reliquary wherein the venerated cloth reposed. At risk to their own personal safety, two unidentified Franciscans, plus one or two laymen, plunged into the fiery chapel, broke the locks, and succeeded in removing the shroud to safety.[10]

A blob of molten silver from the reliquary's lining had penetrated the cloth's forty-eight folds, leaving symmetrical holes and scorches to disfigure the shroud. The smoldering cloth was doused with water, and water stains remain visible today (between the two images and in the region of the knees as well as the chest and back). "Yet," says Ian Wilson, "seemingly miraculously, the image itself had scarcely been touched."[11] For the credulous, perhaps that is one way of putting it.

Until the worst of the burn holes were rather crudely patched, the shroud was withheld from view. This spawned rumors that the shroud had been destroyed and even that it had been replaced by a copy. So persistent were the rumors that at the request of Duke Charles III the Pope appointed a commission that looked into the matter and officially denied the rumors.[12]

Subsequently, in April of 1534, four nuns of the Poor Clare Convent in Chambéry sewed a backing piece of holland cloth onto the shroud and stitched twenty-two patches cut from an altar cloth over the more seriously burned areas. The nuns returned the patched cloth on May 2, along with a generally accurate descriptive report they had drafted. However, this stated in part that the two body images seen on the front of the cloth were almost as visible on the back—a fact now discounted.[13]

When the shroud was again placed on view the rumors of its destruction and replacement quieted, although in recent years one expert who actually examined the shroud concluded the image was the work of an artist and argued that the shroud is not the original cloth of Lirey but dates from a later period.[14] The expert did, however, concede it is the same one which underwent the 1532 fire. (Evidence for this comes from a copy dated 1516; see Chapter 10.)

That aside (and we will continue to assume the repaired cloth is identical to the Lirey one), the next events in the shroud's history are minor ones. In 1535 it was taken to Piedmont and then to Turin, where it was exhibited. It was displayed in Milan the following year. But now the shroud was threatened by invading French troops. For safety, the supposed palladium was spirited away to Vercelli, then taken between various sanctuaries, from Vercelli to Nice, then back to Vercelli in 1449. In 1553, while Vercelli was being sacked by the French, the shroud was hidden away in the home of a church canon.[15]

Returned to Chambéry in 1561, heralded by torches and trumpets, the shroud was once again exhibited on the high altar of the restored Sainte Chapelle of the Holy Shroud. Its silver-lined reliquary having been destroyed during the 1532 fire, the shroud was kept during this period in an iron box, being removed only for an occasional exhibition, such as that for a new duchess in 1566.

By now, Duke Emmanuel Philibert of Savoy had begun to see that Turin would make a far more suitable capital for the expanded Savoy realm than Chambéry. Wilson says that the "astute" Duke "needed the right sort of excuse" to transfer the shroud to Turin and that this came in the person of St. Charles Borromeo. Borromeo, Archbishop of Milan, had supposedly vowed (during a plague in Milan) to make a pilgrimage on foot to the shrine of the Holy Shroud. Now in a "shrewd move,"[16] the Duke was able to accomplish his political goal by transferring the shroud to Turin on the pretext of an act of kindliness toward the venerable Archbishop. If the shroud did not possess palladian powers it did carry political clout, and on September 14, 1578, the transfer was made. Less than a month later, on October 10, Borromeo walked into Turin and venerated what he thought was the Holy Shroud of Christ. On seeing it, he wept.[17]

Turin became the shroud's permanent home. It has remained in Turin until today, except for a period (1939-1946) during World War II when it was lodged for safekeeping in the remote Abbey of Monte Vergine (Avellino), a Benedictine monastery in the mountains of southern Italy.[18]

During the seventeenth century the shroud continued to be exhibited on occasion in Turin. Engravings from this period depict the shroud as a battle standard, waving above the Duke (Amadeus) and Duchess of Savoy and bearing the inscription, "In this sign, conquer." (This is an extention of the shroud's reputed palladian powers. It was later described, in 1778, as a "preservative against all kinds of accidents," and Wilson states, "subsequently in engravings it became associated with the preservation of the whole city of Turin.")[19]

The shroud continued to be regarded generally as authentic, although the church never proclaimed it as such. But notes of skepticism, or at least of extreme caution, were sounded. For example, in Rome in 1670, the Congregation of Indulgences granted to shroud pilgrims a plenary indulgence, *"not for venerating the cloth as the true Shroud of Christ,* but rather for meditating on his Passion, especially his death and burial."[20] [Emphasis added.] One wonders if the Congregation had been aware of Clement's 1389 decree, which the indulgence strongly echoed.

Late in the seventeenth century, on June 1, 1694, the shroud was placed in its present shrine in the Turin Cathedral of St. John the Baptist, a black marble chapel designed by the architect Guarino Guarini. At this time the shroud was provided with a new backing cloth and some additional patches were applied.[21]

Few exhibitions of the shroud were held during the eighteenth century, apparently in the belief that the cloth would be damaged by excessive handling. However, it was displayed in 1750 by the Duke Victor Amadeus III for his royal wedding.

There were five exhibitions in the nineteenth century, the last occurring in 1898, when the shroud was photographed for the first time. Initially Umberto I of the House of Savoy, King of Italy, and hereditary owner of the heirloom, refused to allow photographing of the shroud "on the grounds," states Humber, "that reproducing the sacred object in such a way would diminish the reverence and devotion accorded the relic."[22]

But eventually Umberto grudgingly acquiesced, with the stipulation that the photographic work not interfere with the exhibition. This was a rather severe limitation; but the person chosen for the task—a politician and self-taught amateur photographer named Secondo Pia—came prepared. Using a collapsible scaffold and floodlights diffused by ground-glass screening, Pia made a first abortive attempt on May 25. When the heat from the floodlights shattered the glass screens, Pia was forced to pack up and await his second (and final) opportunity.

To complicate matters, the Princess Clotilde now insisted the shroud be protected with a glass cover that produced glaring reflections. Nevertheless, on May 28, Pia succeeded in making two exposures—one of fourteen minutes' duration and another of twenty minutes. He rushed home to his darkroom.

As he developed his glass plates and held one to the light, Pia made a startling discovery. The image on the shroud became strikingly "lifelike": The negative plate had transformed the negative imprint on the shroud into a positive image. Pia was later to say he was so shocked he almost dropped the plate.[23]

Pia's photographs sparked new controversy over the shroud, with proponents claiming no artist—certainly none working before the invention of photography—could have produced such negative images. That claim would continue until recent times; but at the turn of the century, as noted in Chapter 1, Canon Chevalier rediscovered the ancient documents—the d'Arcis memorandum, the decrees from Pope Clement VII, and the other papers—that stated the shroud was a "representation," the work of an artist who had confessed to having "cunningly painted" the images.

At about the same time a pair described as "the believer and the agnostic"[24] teamed up and concocted a "theory" they believed proved the image on the shroud was authentic. This was the so-called "vaporograph" theory, which held that body vapors from the dead Jesus had interacted with spices on the cloth to produce a vapor photo or "vaporograph." (This now discredited hypothesis will be discussed in a later chapter.) The two announced their opinions in 1902.

The shroud has thus far been exhibited only four times in this century, the first for twenty days in 1931, when a new set of photographs was made by a professional photographer named Giuseppe Enrie. To enhance the faint image, Enrie used a yellow filter and orthochromatic (rather than panchromatic) film. While producing bold contrast, it also, of course, produced tonal distortions.[25] It was exhibited for a similar length of time in 1933 at the request of Pope Pius XI. It would not be placed on public view again until four decades later.

But in 1969 it was the subject of some clandestine activities. A secret commission had been formed to examine the shroud and, when a disgruntled sindonologist leaked this fact to the press, it was denied by Turin church authorities, who subsequently "were forced to admit what they had previously denied."[26]

In 1973, at the time of an exhibition for television only, the commission secretly removed samples from the shroud, which were subsequently tested at various laboratories. The commission finally published its report in 1976. The "blood" on the shroud had failed the sophisticated forensic tests, and the report contained strong suggestions that the shroud was the work of an artist. Astonishingly, the International Center of Sindonology— which, Humber says, "is tantamount to the authority that appointed the commission in the first place"[27]—issued a rebuttal report. (The commission's findings will be discussed later in detail.)

The most recent public exposition of the shroud, lasting forty-two days, during which time Pope John Paul I was elected and died, began August 26, 1978. During October a team of scientists known as the Shroud of Turin Research Project (STURP) conducted a five-day examination and obtained samples for additional tests by the famed microanalyst, Dr. Walter C. McCrone. He concluded that the shroud image had been rendered in tempera paint and that, most probably, the image was the work of a medieval artist. The 1389 memorandum of Bishop d'Arcis, alleging the artist had confessed, had been verified by modern science. It had taken almost six centuries.

# 3

# The Jewish Burial of Jesus

What Bishop d'Arcis termed "the twofold image of one man" on the shroud is suggestive of a body having been wrapped in the cloth. The placement of the figures would indicate that the "body" had been placed on its back on one half of the fourteen-foot length of linen, and then the cloth had been folded (over the head) to cover the front of the body. This under-and-over concept of how the crucified Christ was wrapped for burial is illustrated in a sixteenth-century painting[1] based on the shroud. But can this concept be reconciled with historical evidence and gospel narratives?

Two authenticity advocates, Stevenson and Habermas, concede: "If the Shroud is the actual burial garment of Jesus, then it should be consistent with the New Testament texts. This condition must satisfied before anyone can identify the cloth as Jesus' burial garment."[2]

Of the four gospels, the first three—Matthew, Mark, and Luke—are termed "synoptic" gospels[3] because of their rather close correspondence. (The more theological fourth gospel, John, concentrates on Jesus' ministry in Jerusalem.) Mark, probably the earliest written,[4] states that Joseph of Arimathea asked for and received custody of the body of Jesus: "And he bought fine linen, and took him down, and wrapped him in the linen, and laid him in a sepulchre." (Mark 15:46). Luke 23:53 follows Mark almost verbatim. Matthew 27:59 states the body was wrapped "in a clean linen cloth."

The word used in the synoptics for "linen" or "linen cloth" is *sindon,* ancient Greek for "a linen cloth which could be used for any purpose, including burial."[5] For example, *sindon* is used for the garment worn (like a robe) by the "young man" who fled Gethsemane at Jesus' arrest (Mark 14:51–52).[6] As another instance, in the Old Testament (Judges 14:12), Samson uses the word to describe a linen garment that would be worn with a coat or tunic.[7] A tunic, possibly with a *sindon* wrapped around it, is known to have been used for burial by Coptic Christians in Egypt towards the end of the first century. The body was then "wound mummy-style with ribbons of cloth."[8] Trunks full of such burial tunics are found in the Gayet collection in the Coptic section of the Louvre in Paris. Included with the tunics are some "small napkin-sized pieces of cloth" described as "the size of facecloths."[9] This is most suggestive in light of the Gospel of John.

John gives the fullest account of Jesus' burial. He states that Joseph of Arimathea and Nicodemus (who "brought a mixture of myrrh and aloes, about an hundred pound weight") "took...the body of Jesus, and wound it in *linen clothes* with the spices, as the manner of the Jews is to bury." (John 19:40; emphasis added.)

Later, after the tomb is found empty, John again refers in the plural to "linen clothes." He says that Simon Peter and "the other disciple, whom Jesus loved," came to the entrance; then Peter "went into the sepulcher, and seeth the linen clothes lie, and the napkin, that was about his head, not lying with the linen clothes, but wrapped together in a place by itself." (John 20:6–7)

John clearly refers to multiple burial garments, using the plural *othonia.* These are generally understood by biblical scholars to be "strips of linen cloth," or "wrappings" or "linen bandages"—indicating that the body was wrapped mummy-style. According to one scholarly source, the "bandages" would be "wound fold upon fold round the body."[10] Some have thought that the *sindon,* or sheet, was torn into strips for this purpose.[11] Humber disagrees, although he concedes such a theory "does reconcile with the Synoptics, but it destroys the authenticity of the Shroud."[12]

Another possibility is that *othonia* could include a *sindon,* wound over (as in the case of the Coptic burials) "mummy-style with ribbons of cloth." We know that various burial garments were used by the early Christians. As Barbet says:

> The custom of the first Christians, which must have been inspired by that of the Jews, is confirmed for us by the *Acta Martyrum,* where we always find references to shrouds, linen fabrics, plain linen garments or others more or less ornamented.... In the *loculi* of the catacombs one finds linen cloths, cloths dyed purple, figured and ornamented fabrics and silks, cloth of gold and precious garments, such as those in which St. Cecilia is clothed in the cemetery of Domitilla.[13]

Although Luke uses the singular *sindon,* he later states (24:12) that upon coming to the empty tomb Peter "beheld the linen clothes laid by themselves." Luke here uses the plural *othonia,* thus reinforcing John's account.

To return to the "napkin" mentioned by John—the Greek word he employs is *sudarium* ("sweat cloth"), which means a handkerchief or napkin, and "no other meaning is attributed to it in either Greek or Latin, from which the Greeks took the word."[14] This seems identical to the Coptic Christians' "small napkin-sized pieces of cloth," which were "the size of facecloths." Undoubtedly they were used as such. That the *sudarium* refers to a face veil in John is clear from his statement that the napkin "was about his [Jesus] head" and, in the burial of Lazarus (John 11:44) "his face was bound about with a napkin."

John states that Jesus was buried "as the manner of the Jews is to bury." The facecloth or "napkin" (*sudarium*) is known to have been used in ancient Jewish burial practice. The use of a handkerchief to cover the face is specifically mentioned in the Mishnah (the first part of the Jewish Talmud) about 200 A.D. As Humber rightly notes: "Here, as elsewhere in the Mishnah, it is difficult to apply a time-frame to the information given, but it is safe to assume that the practice was extant at the time of Jesus' death."[15] That it was indeed so is apparent from John's specific statement to that effect. His gospel was written sometime between 90 and 150. Moreover, some argue—on the basis of his "accurate acquaintance with Jewish laws, customs, and opinions," his "rather Hebraic than Greek" style and syntax, and his occasionally demonstrated "knowledge of the original Hebrew" of the Old Testament—that John was himself a Palestinian Jew.[16] At the least, it seems clear that he was quite familiar with Jewish customs, including those pertaining to burial.

The matter of the facecloth is a crucial one, as two skeptical clergymen, Josh McDowell and Don Stewart, observe:

> John 20:5-7 clearly indicates there was a separate piece wrapped about Christ's head. It was found by itself apart from the body wrappings. However, the cloth of Turin *depicts a face on the sheet* as well as the rest of the body. [Emphasis added.][17]

And Barbet notes:

> The objection has for a long time been made and is still being made that this veil, when laid over the face of Jesus, would have prevented the formation of this imprint on the shroud when placed over it.[18]

Barbet, however, speculated that the image of Christ might have been projected through the veil and onto the "shroud"—without, apparently, causing the face image to appear lighter than the remaining body image.

Some sindonologists, such as the Rev. John A. T. Robinson of Trinity College, shrewdly attempt to circumvent the evidence of the facecloth by imagining it rolled up and thus converted into a chin-band.[19] But *sudarium* never meant anything of the sort; as a "sweat cloth" it has always indicated a handkerchief or napkin, facecloth or veil—never a jaw-band. The Rev. Bernard Orchard concedes that a chin- or jaw-band could have been one of the *othonia*. "But," he adds, "I do not think that the 'jaw-band' was the sudarion. I think that Robinson's imagination is here running away with itself!"[20]

Some sindonologists, including Robinson, imagine they can see indications of a chin-band in the spaces on either side of the face on the shroud. But this effect is due merely to a differently toned stripe of the herringbone-weave cloth, which says the report of the 1978 investigation, "has been mistakenly taken as evidence for a chin band." (A footnote to the report at this point gives references to Robinson and Barbet.)[21]

The gospel accounts of how Jesus' and Lazarus' bodies were wrapped offer further evidence against the under-and-over draping concept mandated by the double image on the shroud. In the case of Lazarus (related only by John), as well as that of Jesus, John uses the verb *deo,* meaning " 'to bind' or 'tie' with the result of imprisonment." He states that Lazarus was "bound hand and foot with graveclothes." In describing Jesus' burial, Matthew and Luke use the verb *entulisso,* which means "to wrap (up), to fold"; and Mark employs *eneileo,* "which connotes to wrap up, to confine."[22]

But if Jesus was "bound" with "strips of linen cloths," perhaps tied over a burial garment, then why would a fourteenth-century forger—who obviously must have relied on the gospel narratives for many of his details (for example, the marks of scourging)—depict the "twofold image" of Jesus on a single length of linen? For an answer we need only take a look at the apocryphal references to the reputed preservation of Jesus' burial garments. (See also Chapter 5.)

The concept of what these consisted of evolved over the centuries preceding the Middle Ages. An account dated about 570 referred to Christ's *sudarium* (facecloth) without any mention of a facial imprint; in later centuries there were eight-foot-long linen cloths, which were represented as *sindons*—each alleged to be the very shroud of Christ. By the twelfth century, in certain artistic Lamentation and Deposition scenes (some done in fresco), there was depicted "a large double-length piece of linen, obviously intended," says Wilson, "to envelop the body over the head, a cloth we would unhesitatingly identify as a shroud."[23] Thus the stage was set—no matter how much a misconception—for the creation of a "shroud" like the cloth of Turin. The evidence therefore argues against the cloth being the authentic burial garment of Jesus, dating from the first century, but rather suggests a date in the twelfth- to fourteenth-century range.

So does the nature of the cloth itself. The official commission

(1969–1976) conducted secret examinations of the shroud and actually removed several threads, along with two small pieces (one 13 x 40 mm. and one 10 x 40 mm.). Under microscopic examination, Professor Gilbert Raes of the Ghent Institute of Textile Technology discovered (among the linen fibers of the main fabric) minute traces of cotton. This suggested the shroud had been woven on a loom that had previously been used to weave cotton cloth.[24] On the basis of this minor finding, Stevenson and Habermas rush to a conclusion: "This discovery helped pinpoint the location of the Shroud's manufacture: Cotton is not grown in Europe, but it grows abundantly in the Middle East."[25]

However, at least as early as the thirteenth century, cotton cloth was *manufactured* in France (as well as in Italy and Flanders). Earlier, it had been imported from India. Cloth markets were held as part of the annual Hot Fair of Troyes, the most important of the six Champagne fairs; and "cloth halls" persisted in Troyes until a serious fire in 1524 destroyed the commercial quarter of the city. Locally made linen and cotton cloth were very much in evidence in this diocese, where the shroud first came to light.[26] The cotton fibers Professor Raes found on the shroud supposedly "correspond to the species *Gossypium herbacium* which is characteristic of the Middle East," says Wilson, who nevertheless concedes: "Of course, it is possible that a fourteenth-century Western forger might have obtained a piece of genuine Middle Eastern cloth for his purpose, East-West trade being reasonably well developed at the time."[27] Indeed, goods from the East went via Constantinople to Troyes.[28]

The weave of the cloth of Turin is a three-to-one twill, striped in the herringbone pattern. This is suspect in itself, since most linens of Jesus's time—whether Roman, Egyptian, or Palestinian—were plain weave. Moreover we have the testimony of Rev. David Sox, the knowledgeable former secretary of the British Society for the Turin Shroud (who resigned when new evidence persuaded him the shroud of Turin is a forgery).

> The problem with the weave is that, to date, archeologically, there are no examples of the kind of weave we have in the Shroud...in any artifacts earlier than the late middle ages except for one or two *variations* of that weave. *All* of the ancient Egyptian linens extant are different. *All* of the extant Palestinian linen, including the wrappings from the Dead Sea Scrolls, is of a regular weave—quite different from the shroud.[29]

Very few examples of Palestinian cloth do in fact exist, due to the excessive humidity of the climate.[30] Yet the shroud seems to be in a rather amazing state of preservation despite its reputed age of nearly 2000 years. On viewing the shroud, Wilson stated: "The linen, although ivory-colored with age, was still surprisingly clean looking, even to the extent of a damasklike surface sheen." He adds, "In the areas untouched by the ravages of history [the weave] was in remarkably good condition."[31] Since most of the "ravages" are the result of the 1532 fire, it would seem that the cloth was not noticeably damaged when it first appeared at Lirey, about 1357, although it was then reputed to be thirteen centuries old.

Then there is the related problem of so large a piece of ancient linen having survived. Sox observes:

> There are lots of samples much older than 2,000 years. Linen, which is essentially cellulose, is an extremely durable material. But what *is* a problem is that you just don't find anything quite the size of the Shroud except for the Egyptian mummy wrappings—certainly nothing that measures fourteen feet, the size of the Shroud. That's a helluva lot of linen! What I'm suggesting is that it's just too large to be convincing, too much to have been kept intact for so long.[32]

The problem of so large a cloth having survived is magnified by the fact that such a shroud, as a Christian religious cloth, would have been the target both of pillaging armies and of the Iconoclasts (723-842), who destroyed countless religious works, relics, and even other miraculous "portraits" of Christ. (See Chapter 4.) Thus, taken together, it would seem that the weave and the quantity of such well-preserved fabric are more consistent with an age of six centuries, and not twenty. One can only agree with Wilson: "On the face of it, the very idea that the linen cloth in which Jesus Christ was wrapped in the tomb should have survived to this day would seem incredible."[33]

One intriguing point of evidence concerns the "side strip," an 8- to 9-centimeter-wide piece of linen sewn along one side of the shroud. This strip is of identical weave to that of the main portion of the cloth, although the threads seem somewhat different in size and no traces of cotton were found (at least in the tiny piece examined). What is interesting is that, as Professor Silvio Curto of the commmission noted, the images on the shroud would be off-center without the side strip. And since the two pieces of fabric are so similar, it would appear that the piece was sewn on approximately contemporaneous with the origin of the shroud. The most likely explanation of this, Wilson argues, is that the side strip was sewn on specifically "in order to balance the image on the cloth."[34] (It would be easy for an artist to match the cloth of a new work he had produced, but much more difficult for someone else at a later period.) It seems unlikely that the strip would be added *before* the image was produced—whether the cloth actually served as a shroud or was utilized by an artist for a representation of the same.

The width of the main piece would have been quite ample in either case.

To return to John's account of Jesus' burial: his statement that Jesus was buried in the customary Jewish manner would have meant a ritualistic washing of the body, followed by anointment. Both the washing and the anointing are expressly mandated by the Mishnah (although it does not state the exact ointments or spices).[35] In Acts 9:37 we find a mention of the ritualistic pre-burial washing of the deceased.

However, the "body" imprinted on the shroud was not washed. This is evident, for example, from the dried "blood" (as on the arms), a fact with which most sindonologists agree. Admits Wilson, "Only on the view that Jesus was not washed can the authenticity of the Turin Shroud be upheld."[36] He and other pro-authenticity writers attempt to dismiss this important evidence by suggesting that there was insufficient time for Jesus' body to be washed before the Sabbath and that the gospel writers were simply reluctant to admit the fact.

But McDowell and Stewart call such conclusions

> ...erroneous at best. The idea of there not being time to wash the body clean with water because of the approaching sabbath is equally weak because the Scripture says they still had time to anoint the body with over a hundred pounds of spices. This is also made clear in the fact that a body could indeed be washed and anointed on the sabbath.[37]

McDowell and Stewart here quote from the Mishnah: "The corpse may, however, be washed and anointed on the sabbath, provided the limbs be not strained out of joint."[38]

The spices represent another scriptural argument against authenticity, since John says about "an hundred pound weight" was brought (not all of it necessarily used) and the body was wound "in linen clothes with the spices" (John 19:39–40). But many sindonologists discount John since the anointing with spices would only have taken place after the body was first washed. They prefer instead to look to the synoptics, where Luke (23:55–56) and Mark (16:1)—but not Matthew—says that at the end of the Sabbath Mary Magdalene and Mary, the mother of James, were carrying spices to the tomb when they discovered the stone rolled away. Some biblical scholars argue there is not necessarily a disagreement between John and the synoptics, since the women might not have known that Joseph and Nicodemus had already performed the anointing, or they might have wished to perform a further, more complete embalming.[39]

While Mark refers simply to "sweet spices" and Luke to "spices and ointments," John specifically states that a mixture of myrrh and aloes was used for the anointing. Although conceding that if the body was not washed there would be no anointing, Wilson offers a clever rationalization for the myrrh and aloes of John. He suggests the spices were "dry blocks of aromatics packed around the body as antiputrefacients." (He argues that such an arrangement could further "account for the lack of distortion of the body image, which has always been one of the Shroud's mysteries."[40]) But again, what John says is that the body was wound in the burial clothes "*with* the spices." Of course the sindonologists are free to question John's credibility on the details of the burial if they wish, although one should then wonder why they are eager to accept him in other matters, notably that of the lance wound (mentioned in John but absent from the synoptics). In any case neither the commission scientists, nor those of the 1978 investigation by the Shroud of Turin Research Project (STURP), reported finding myrrh or aloes on the shroud. (We shall return to this matter in later chapters.)

There is yet another argument against the shroud's being authentic, if one accepts John's statement that Jesus was buried in accordance with Jewish custom. This would have meant, according to the *Code of Jewish Law*, that Jesus' hair and beard would have been shaved off—something clearly not done to the "man in the shroud." Monsignor Giulio Ricci, an ardent sindonologist who argues the case for "a hurried burial rite," states:

> For a normal burial on the other hand, a shroud of just over 3 meters was sufficient to wrap round the body (already washed 7 times, beard and hair completely shaven, sprinkled with spices and dressed in its clothes), leaving the face bare; the latter would be suitably covered at the last moment with a napkin costing a shekel.

Yet, despite the supposed hasty burial, Ricci can still speak of the (unmatted) hair and beard "which someone had lovingly combed at the end of that first Good Friday."[41]

If the sindonologists have attempted to sweep aside the evidence from the Gospel of John that argues against the authenticity of the Turin cloth, at least one priest believes he has found proof the shroud is authentic. The Rev. Francis Filas of Chicago thinks he can see evidence of "coins" over the eyes of the figure on the shroud—or at least one eye, the right eye of the figure. Using enhanced, high-contrast photographs (which therefore contain serious tonal distortions), Filas believes he can make out the impression of a coin minted by Pontius Pilate about 29-32 A.D.[42] But, says Sox:

> Unfortunately, most experts say that coins over the eyes is more likely a pagan, rather than a Jewish, burial practice. When presented with the photographs upon which all this hoopla in the press was based, one scientist—who shall remain nameless—said, "Yes, and if you look a little more closely, in the upper right hand corner, you can see Donald Duck...and, why, over there, on the left, is Mickey Mouse.

Sox adds:

> As Dr. Ray Rogers [a STURP scientist] has pointed out, there are examples
> of extraneous markings on the image...which probably allow a person to see
> what he wants to see. There's no question in my mind but what the Shroud
> has caused some people to lose their balance—especially journalists.[43]

A shroud critic, Dr. Marvin M. Mueller of the Los Alamos National
Laboratory, has made a study of Filas' claims, has himself examined the
photographs under magnification, and concludes: "The magnified weave patterns in the image areas function somewhat as a Rorschach test—one sees
what one wants to see."[44]

In examining the compatibility (or rather lack thereof) of the shroud
with the New Testament, one must finally place considerable weight on what
the gospels, the Acts of the Apostles, and the other New Testament texts
*omit*: namely, any reference whatsoever to such an amazing imprint being
found on Jesus' burial clothes. As Pierre d'Arcis stated in his memorandum
to the Pope, reporting on the investigations which he and Henri de Poitiers
had conducted, there had been an obvious reason to investigate:

> For many theologians and other wise persons declared that this could not be
> the real shroud of our Lord having the Saviour's likeness thus imprinted upon
> it, since the holy Gospel made no mention of any such imprint, while, if it
> had been true, it was quite unlikely that the holy Evangelists would have omit-
> ted to record it, or that the fact should have remained hidden until the pres-
> ent time.

Strongly echoing the view of the two bishops, Reverends McDowell and
Stewart question whether the apostles and early Christians—who gave "personal testimony of Christ's resurrection appearances in the most adverse
situations"—would fail to mention such a remarkable cloth. They find such
a notion "totally unthinkable."[45]

# 4

# Self-Portraits of Christ?

The questionable provenance of the shroud of Turin has been a continual embarrassment to sindonologists, particularly in light of the claim by Bishop Pierre d'Arcis that a fourteenth-century forger "cunningly painted" the double image of Jesus' body. They have therefore attempted to explain away the 1300-year silence in the historical record. Hence, Stevenson and Habermas state in *Verdict on the Shroud* (a pro-authenticity work):

> They have developed evidence for what has become known as the "iconographic theory," the theory that the Shroud was known to artists as early as the sixth century, and that it inspired the conventional likeness of Christ.[1]

Certainly the image of the "man of the shroud" has always been recognized as seemingly that of Jesus—the Christ of the New Testament. Not only the bearded visage (familiar from countless paintings) but also the flagellation marks and crucifixion details (the "wounds" in the hands, feet, and side, and the marks from a "crown of thorns") have prompted the identification of the figure as Jesus.

Although Bishop d'Arcis emphatically believed the shroud a fake, his memorandum tacitly recognized that the image represented "the whole likeness of the Saviour" with the supposed "wounds which He bore." Furthermore, all the available evidence indicates that pilgrims who viewed the cloth at Lirey and elsewhere found no difficulty in equating what they saw with the appearance of Jesus as they had come to know it. Pope Clement VII described the touted shroud as a "representation." Apparently it was an acceptable one.

Stevenson and Habermas state: "People immediately recognize this [a 3-D recreation of the face on the shroud] as the face of Christ—precisely because it *is* the standard face of Jesus in art."[2] Wilson, a major proponent of the "iconographic theory" agrees and adds:

> Even alone this raised intriguing questions. If the Shroud was a forgery, the compatibility was of no special significance because one could presume that the forger merely copied the conventional likeness.[3]

Skeptics *do* so presume — all the more because of the cloth's lack of provenance until the mid-fourteenth century, plus the reported confession of "the artist who had painted it," and the resemblance of the figure to medieval Gothic art (with some Byzantine influence). Still, Wilson continues:

> But if the Shroud was genuine, the fact that there was such a close similarity between its likeness and that in art suggested that somehow, somewhere its existence had been known in the early centuries, and if known, had most likely been documented.

"Could one," Wilson asked, "possibly tell by tracing the likeness back through the centuries where and what the Shroud may have been?"

In attempting to answer this question, we should remember, first of all, that there is no clue to the physical appearance of Jesus in the gospels or, for that matter, anywhere in the New Testament or contemporary histories. As St. Augustine lamented in the early fifth century — although noting there were many representations of Christ — "we do not know of his external appearance, nor that of his mother."[4] Insofar as the New Testament is concerned, Jesus may have been neither tall nor bearded nor impressive in appearance — as he is represented on the shroud of Turin; on the contrary he may well have been short, beardless, and unimposing. Indeed, in an Old Testament prophecy of the coming of the Messiah, Isaiah wrote:

> He hath no form nor comeliness; and when we see him, there is no beauty that we should desire him.
> He is despised and rejected of men; a man of sorrows, and acquainted with grief: and we hid as it were our faces from him; he was despised, and we esteemed him not. (Isaiah 53:2–3)

Many early Christian writers therefore thought Christ ugly; but others argued that Isaiah was surely referring to the appearance of the *crucified* Jesus, and they cited another passage they believed prophetic: "Thou art fairer than the children of men: grace is poured into thy lips: therefore God hath blessed thee for ever." (Psalms 45:2)

With such disparate, putative prophesies, and a lack of gospel description, it is not surprising that we find varying conceptual portraits of Jesus from the early centuries. Another factor may have played a part in this, namely the Judaic prohibition against graven images: "Thou shalt not make unto thee any graven image, or any likeness of any thing that is in heaven above, or that is in the earth beneath, or that is in the water under the earth. Thou shalt not bow down thyself to them...." (Exodus 20:4–5)

Since this prohibition seems to have carried over into very early Christianity, it may help explain the paucity of Christ images.

Indeed, we must look to the middle of the third century for the earliest known representation of Jesus: This is a painting done in fresco, representing him as young, beardless, and with cropped hair. There are other similar representations. David Sox states, "The earliest portrayals of Jesus in Christian art were generally of an Apollo or young shepherd type."[5] This type of portrayal continued into the fourth and fifth centuries.

But from approximately the same time, that is, from the third and fourth centuries, the Apollo-type Christ image was paralleled by a more Semitic representation—with long, flowing hair and beard, large, accentuated eyes, and a prominent nose. Eventually this concept prevailed—throughout the Byzantine empire and later in Europe—as a matter of rigid artistic convention. According to Marcello Craveri in *The Life of Jesus:*

> To explain how after so many centuries it was possible to make an authentic portrait of the Savior, it was said that there had always been a traditional secret picture composed by none other than Luke. The first to tell of this legend was Andrew, metropolitan of Crete, in 710. Backed up by such contentions, portraits of Jesus multiplied to such an extent that only a few years later Emperor Leo III the Isaurian had to order a harsh persecution against images, which led to passionate debates on the legitimacy of portraying Jesus and the danger of falling into heathen idolatry.[6]

There also appeared, as early as the sixth century, certain images of Jesus reputed to be *acheiropoietos,* or "not made with hands."[7] There were several versions of these, and as many legends to account for their supposedly miraculous origin.

One of the legends concerns the "Image of Edessa." The story is related in a mid-fourth-century Syriac manuscript, *The Doctrine of Addai,*[8] which tells how a leprosy-afflicted King Abgar of Edessa (now Urfa, in southcentral Turkey) supposedly sent a messenger named Ananias to deliver a letter to Jesus. In the letter[9] Abgar sends "greetings to Jesus the Savior who has come to light as a good physician in the city of Jerusalem," and who, he has heard, "can make the blind see, the lame walk...heal those who are tortured by chronic illnesses, and...raise the dead." Abgar decides, he says to Jesus, that either Jesus is God himself or the Son of God, and so he entreats Jesus to "come to me and cure me of my disease." He notes that he has heard of the Jews' plan to harm Jesus and adds, "I have a very small city, but it is stately and will be sufficient for us both to live in peace."

Abgar, so the story goes, instructed Ananias that if he were unable to persuade Jesus to return with him to Edessa, he was to bring back a portrait instead. But while Ananias sat on a rock drawing the portrait, Jesus summoned him, divining his mission and the fact of the letter Ananias carried. After reading it, Jesus responded with a letter of his own, writing, "Blessed are you, Abgar, in that you believed in me without having actually seen me." Jesus said that, while he must fulfill his mission on earth, he would later send one of his disciples to cure Abgar's suffering and to "also provide your city with a sufficient defence to keep all your enemies from taking it." After entrusting the letter to Ananias,

> The Savior then washed his face in water, wiped off the moisture that was left on the towel that was given to him, and in some divine and inexpressible manner had his own likeness impressed on it.[10]

Jesus gave Ananias the towel to present to Abgar as "consolation" for his disease.

An official account[11] of the Image (dating from the tenth century), which relates the above legend, notes: "there is another story about this [cloth] which is neither incredible nor short of reliable witnesses." In this second version, the image is impressed with Jesus' bloody sweat during his agony in the garden of Gethsemane (Luke 22:44):

> They say that when Christ was about to go voluntarily to death he was seen to reveal his human weakness, feel anguish, and pray. According to the Evangelist, sweat dropped from him like drops of blood. Then they say he took this piece of cloth which we see now from one of the disciples and wiped off the drops of sweat on it. At once the still-visible impression of that divine face was produced.[12]

The tale continues with Jesus giving the cloth to Thomas for safekeeping until after Jesus had ascended into heaven, at which time "the divine portrait of Christ's face" was to be taken by Thaddaeus to King Abgar. Subsequently, Abgar supposedly touched the magical cloth to the afflicted parts of his body and was cleansed of his leprosy.

Sir Steven Runciman denounces both versions of the story as apocryphal:

> It is easy to show that the story of Abgar and Jesus as we now have it is untrue, that the letters contain phrases copied from the gospels and are framed according to the dictates of later theology.

He adds, rather lamely, "But that does not necessarily invalidate the tradition on which the story was based...."[13] Be that as it may, there is yet a later version of the proliferating tale. The impressed cloth in this version is distinguished from the Image of Edessa (later called the Mandylion) as "Veronica's Veil."

Veronica, according to legend, was a pious woman of Jerusalem, who was so moved to pity at witnessing Jesus struggling with his cross to Golgotha that she wiped his face with her veil (or kerchief) and thereby obtained his portrait imprinted with his bloody sweat.[14] (In some versions Veronica gives the veil to Jesus so that he might wipe his brow, and he, pleased at such an offering, miraculously imprints his face upon it.[15])

Not surprising, there were many of these figured veils, known as "veronicas"—the term seems to have been a corruption of the words *vera icon* (true image).[16] (In what appears to be a further corruption, dating from the fifteenth century, the cloth is sometimes referred to as "the holy vernicle [sic] of Rome."[17]) These "veronicas" were, states Humber, "supposedly miraculous, but, in fact, painted."[18]

The Veronica tradition, which dates from the fourteenth century, derives from the Edessan one, which has been traced to an account (about 325) by Bishop Eusebius.[19] This mentions the Abgar/Jesus correspondence and (instead of Veronica) the woman with the "issue of blood" who was cured when she touched Jesus' garment (Mark 5:25–34; Matthew 9:20–22; Luke 8:43–48). But Eusebius *omits the figured cloth* from his Abgar/Jesus account, and all accounts of such imprinted veils date from later times—probably the earliest certain reference being the mid-fourth-century *The Doctrine of Addai.*[20]

In one revealing fourth-century text of *The Doctrine of Addai,* the Image of Edessa is described not as of miraculous origin but merely as the work of Hannan (Ananias), who "took and painted a portrait of Jesus in choice paints, and brought it with him to his lord King Abgar."[21]

Nevertheless the Image of Edessa is described in the tenth-century account as "a moist secretion without coloring or painter's art," an "impression" of Jesus' face on "linen cloth" which—such is the way of legend—"eventually became indestructible." (The narrator of the account urges "the realization that concessions must be made to the unintelligibility of God's wisdom.")[22]

Putting aside Ananias' painted portrait of Jesus and returning to the reputedly miraculous ("not-made-with-hands") image—supposedly Christ's own "self-portrait," a designation sometimes applied to the shroud of Turin,[23]—we find conflicting portrayals. To complicate matters, we know of some only from vague written accounts and others from artists' copies (easily distinguishable as such by, for instance, depicting a scene in which

Veronica is holding up the "true" miraculous portrait[24]). And we must realize that we are almost certainly dealing with not one but many "original" images.

As noted earlier, the tenth-century account described the image as "without coloring." Elsewhere in the account it is described as "due to sweat, not pigments" and "it did not consist of earthly colors."[25] But, states Wilson: "On artists' copies of the Mandylion, it [the color] ranges from a sepia monochrome to a rust-brown monochrome, slightly deeper but otherwise virtually identical to the coloring of the image on the Shroud."[26] The monochromatic quality might well be what is meant by "without coloring" and the reddish brown tone could be consistent with the legends that the image was made by a bloody sweat.

In 1907, upon opening the silver reliquary in St. Peter's which supposedly held the Veil of Veronica, Monsignor Joseph Wilpert saw only "a square piece of light-colored material, somewhat faded through age, which bore two faint, irregular rust-brown stains, connected one to the other...."[27] This "relic" had supposedly been seized and lost in the 1527 sacking of Rome by the troops of Charles V.[28] But if that is true, how do we account for the cloth found in the reliquary? Merely an artist's copy? Surely—if we can believe Wilpert's description (and "modern enquiries meet with almost no information from Vatican custodians...."[29])—this object was not an obvious artist's copy (such as the Veronica mentioned earlier). Possibly it was a replacement copy, for as Thomas Humber says,

> Soon the popular demand for more copies representing the "true likeness" of Christ was such that selected artists were allowed or encouraged to make duplications. (There was, conveniently, another tradition supporting the copies: the Image could miraculously duplicate itself.)[30]

But why was the image on this Veronica so crude and indistinct? We can only guess. Possibly most of the pigment had sloughed off, or perhaps the image was initially poorly formed: If an artist had decided upon a more "realistic"—rather than obviously artistic—effect, he might have produced an image by taking an imprint of a real human face. Such an approach can produce hopelessly deformed images—even ones scarcely recognizable as human.[31] Interestingly, the Mandylion viewed in Constantinople in 944 bore an image that was reportedly quite blurred.[32] But, speculation aside, the Veronica of St. Peter's was in the familiar tradition of a small cloth with "rust-brown" imprints.

There may have been one or more exceptions to the tradition of monochromatic, red-brown images: the Holy Face of Laon, at least, known to be one of the early "copies," had some small traces of color in addition to the basic monotonal image; but it has been argued that these were additions made by a later artist.[33] It therefore seems clear that the greater number of the "not-made-with-hands" images were reddish-brown, monochromatic Christ portraits. They were usually—if not always—of the entire head, with flowing hair (in the traditional Byzantine manner), and not merely facial imprints. They were invariably on white cloth, probably fine linen generally, as indicated by the artists' copies as well as the example at St. Peter's.

Unlike the image on the cloth of Lirey, all of the obvious artists' copies show positive images. We do not know if this is the case with the several "original" Mandylion and Veronica images, but if any were made by imprinting actual human faces, or faces from statues, these—however crude the results—would have been negative images. It is a moot point. However, from ancient times (as we shall see in a later chapter) artists have been aware of simple negative images.

In propounding the "iconographic theory," Wilson attempts to equate the shroud with the spurious Mandylion/Veronica images by postulating that the Mandylion *was* the shroud. As evidence, he cites some of the parallels we have already traced; and to the obvious rejoinder that the early Mandylions bore only a facial image, Wilson argues that the "shroud" may have been folded in such a way as to exhibit only the face.[34]

Why would the Shroud of Christ be so exhibited? Wilson thinks it may have been part of a deliberate "deception" to "disguise its nature as 'unclean' burial linen." It may, he speculates, have thus been "made up as a 'portrait' " by being cleverly folded and placed in a frame. He believes that during a time of persecution of Christians in Edessa (about A.D. 57), the disguised "shroud" was hidden for safety "in a niche above Edessa's west gate" where, centuries later (about 525), it was "rediscovered"—according to a much later legend.[35] Even so, he must argue that the "shroud" was not recognized as such until about 1025, when, hypothetically, it was removed from its imagined frame for remounting. Bishop d'Arcis would doubtless have found this conjectural scenario—together with the cloth of Lirey itself—"cunningly painted," but nothing more.

Historians such as Runciman are not persuaded. He observes:

> The Image of Edessa was always described by the Byzantines as a "mandelion," a kerchief, which is quite different from a "sindon." Besides, as we know from the lists of Byzantine relics, they believed that they possessed the Holy Shroud, which is listed separately by them.[36]

Runciman, moreover, believes the Mandylion perished during the French Revolution when, with other booty, the ship carrying it sank at sea. Sox raises several further objections, stating for example, "It seems odd that the disciples would let their Lord's shroud go in a disguised form to a city relatively unknown to them."[37] And there are still further objections, not the least of which is that the Mandylion/Veronica images never show the "blood" from the "crown of thorns," which is clearly visible on the shroud and obviously suggestive of the crucified Christ. Finally, there is not the slightest evidence from examinations of the shroud of Turin to indicate it was fastened into a frame for a thousand years.

In short, to suggest, as Wilson does, that a disguised-as-a-portrait "shroud" served as a "blueprint likeness" that artists copied, is to get the matter backwards. It is much more reasonable to conclude, on the evidence, that the traditional artists' conception of Jesus' appearance served as the model for the fourteenth-century "shroud" and not the other way round.

In fact, there is further suggestive evidence in this regard. While the early Mandylion/Veronica images were face-only portraits, there was a later development which strongly suggests the stage was being set for a double-length image to be created. The evidence is of an evolutionary development from the face-only concept to (in at least two manuscript illustrations of the Mandylion image) one showing a portion of the neck. A thirteenth-century author described the Veronica as depicting Jesus "from the chest upwards." Also, from as early as the twelfth century the Mandylion is sometimes described as bearing "the glorious image of the Lord's face and the length of his whole body," and "the likeness and proportions of the body of the Lord."[38] By the thirteenth century we find this amplification of the story of Jesus giving his portrait to King Abgar:

> For it is handed down from archives of ancient authority that the Lord prostrated himself full length on most white linen, and so by divine power the most beautiful likeness not only of the face, but also of the whole body of the Lord was impressed upon the cloth.[39]

One should remember that these full-length images (obviously front only—not front and back, as on the shroud) were supposed to be of the *living* Jesus; there is no indication that they related to his shroud. Yet as we shall see, the changeover from the body imprint of the living Christ to that of the buried Christ—the latter depicted on a "shroud"—would also be made. The timing is significant: It is in the century just prior to the appearance of the cloth of Lirey.

# 5

# The Shroud as a "Relic"

If genuine, the shroud of Turin would properly be termed a relic. According to the *New Catholic Encyclopedia* relics are "the material remains of a saint or holy person after his death, as well as objects sanctified by contact with his body."[1] Relics include—in addition to hair, blood, skin, and bones—articles of clothing, instruments associated with a martyr's imprisonment or suffering (passion), and so forth. Therefore the shroud is often referred to, by those asserting its authenticity, as a relic since, supposedly, the cloth was in contact with Christ's body in the sepulcher and is believed to bear stains of his actual blood.

There is little or no justification in the Old Testament to support the "cult of relics,"[2] and essentially the same may be said of the New Testament. Indeed, we learn that:

> In the Apocalypse [or Revelation] the author recommends that the faithful and martyrs be left to rest in peace (11:13). Despite this, although the Apostles inherited Jewish diffidence regarding relics, the new converts in the time of St. Paul disputed about objects that belonged to the Apostles and recognized as miraculous agents clothing that they had touched (Acts 19:12).[3]

While there is no mention of the preservation of Christ's relics in the New Testament, there are references to them in certain apocryphal gospels. *The First Gospel of the Infancy of Jesus Christ* claims an "old Hebrew woman" preserved the infant Jesus' foreskin (or perhaps the umbilical; the author is unsure). This was allegedly preserved "in an alabaster box of old oil of spikenard,"[4] said to be the very ointment later used to anoint Jesus' head and feet prior to the events leading up to the crucifixion.

Other passages from the *Gospel of the Infancy* claim that the baby's swaddling clothes worked magic: On one occasion the cloths were instrumental in exorcising a youth's devils, which flew out of his mouth "in the shape of crows and serpents"; in another instance they burst into flames and frightened away a "dreadful dragon" (which was Satan in disguise); it was found that one of the cloths was impervious to fire; and so on.[5] (In the fourteenth century, the supposed swaddling clothes of Christ and a flask of the Virgin's milk were among the incredible relics collected by King Charles V of France for his royal chapel.[6])

In the fourth and fifth centuries,

> ...the veneration of martyr's relics grew as a liturgical cult and received theological justification....The tombs of martyrs were opened, and relics were distributed in the form of *brandea,* or objects that had touched the actual body or bones. These *brandea* were enclosed in little cases [reliquaries] and hung round the neck.[7]

So prevalent had the sale of relics become in the time of St. Augustine (about 400) that he deplored "hypocrites in the garb of monks" for hawking about of the limbs of martyrs," adding skeptically, "if indeed of martyrs."[8] At about the same time, Vigilantius of Toulouse condemned the veneration of relics, which he regarded as pure idolatry, although St. Jerome attempted to defend the cult—in part, on the grounds that reputed miracles were worked by God through saints' relics.[9] According to a recent writer,

> So widespread and insistent was the demand for relics that in the ninth century a specialized corporation was formed in Rome to discover, sell and transport holy relics to all parts of Europe....Roman catacombs were ransacked for old bones, which were duly identified with suitable saints. Some became hydra-headed—a number of churches claimed to have the skull of John the Baptist.[10]

A cathedral in Cologne boasted the skulls of the three Wise Men.[11] Here and there were fingers of St. Paul, St. Andrew, John the Baptist, the doubting Thomas—even one of the Holy Ghost! Teeth attributed to St. Apollonia (allegedly effective in curing toothaches) were beyond counting; a tooth of St. Peter was reputedly discovered resting on his tomb six hundred years after his death; and then there was the gargantuan tooth of St. Paul, though some thought it must have belonged to "one of the monsters of the deep." St. Briocus of Great Britain yielded several relics—two ribs, an arm, and a vetebra—along with a proof of their authenticity. When they were placed in a church at Angers, "they jumped for joy at the honour conferred upon them."[12] The hand of St. William of Oulx, a one-armed peasant, was said to have refused burial by repeatedly pushing itself through the coffin; so the hand was severed and retained as a relic known as the "Angelic Hand." While the relics of St. Paul, Bishop of Leon, were reportedly burnt to powder during the Reformation, a nineteenth-century church somehow obtained his skull, the "entire bone of the right arm" and a finger, all kept in a silver reliquary.

No less than three churches had the corpse of Mary Magdalene; another had, alas, only her foot. An entire cemetery was despoiled in order to provide one monastery with the relics of St. Ursula and her legendary eleven thousand virgin martyrs. "The fact that many of these bones were unquestionably those of men," comments one researcher, "did not affect their curative value."[13] Moreover, we learn that:

> The living bodies of likely future saints were covetously watched by relic mongers; when Thomas Aquinas fell ill and died at a French monastery, his body was decapitated and his flesh boiled away by monks greedy for his bones. It is said that Saint Romuald of Ravenna heard during a visit to France that he was in mortal peril because of the value of his bones — he fled homeward, pretending to be mad.[14]

St. Peter's "relics" were quite prolific. Parings from his toenails existed in remarkable quantity; and there were his chains, "filings" from his chains, and vials of his tears. Someone, somehow, had obtained a vial of sweat from St. Michael when he had contended with Satan. The Vatican still preserves relics of St. Andrew, along with an ornate reliquary for St. Matthew's arm. And there was the gold ring of St. Coletta (or Nicoletta), supposedly sent to her from heaven by St. John the Evangelist as proof that Christ had selected her as his virgin bride. (She also received from John a crucifix, in a small locket of which was a piece of the True Cross.)

The Old Testament prophets were not entirely neglected. There was Moses' rod, Enoch's slippers, and the hem of Joseph's "coat of many colors." An English cathedral had a sprig of the burning bush from which God had instructed Moses. There were various relics of the prophet Daniel.

But much more prolific were "relics" associated with Jesus. We have mentioned his swaddling clothes and foreskin. The latter was preserved in no less than six churches; and at least one survives, kept in a jewel-studded reliquary held aloft by sculpted angels. Preserved also were hay from the manger, some of the babe's hair, his pap-spoon and dish, his navel, his milk teeth, gifts from the Wise Men. There was the cloak with which Joseph had covered the infant at Bethlehem.

Relics of Joseph and Mary were discovered. Found were Joseph's girdle, staff, and hammer, and also various plows fashioned in his carpentry shop and worked on by the young Jesus. Some of Mary's hair was preserved, together with her shirt and vials of her breast milk. So were chips of rock on which a few drops of her milk had fallen, turning the rock white and imbuing it with curative powers. At Loretto, in Italy, pilgrims visited the Holy House in which Mary had lived at the time of the Annunciation; it had, it was claimed, been miraculously transported to its Italian site.

The faithful were able to view, at one time or another, relics commemorating events from Jesus' ministry: a tear shed by him at Lazarus' tomb; his "seamless coat"; one of the vessels in which he changed water to wine; the tail of the ass upon which he rode into Jerusalem; a lock of hair from the woman (Luke 7:44) who washed Christ's feet with her tears and dried his feet with her tresses.

The crucifixion was especially well-represented. The Sainte Chapelle in Paris had the entire crown of thorns, although not the only one, and individual thorns turned up here and there. There were several nails which had been used in the crucifixion, one of which the Empress Helena threw into the Gulf of Venice to quell a storm. A church in Rome still has a slab from the Good Thief's cross. Fragments of the True Cross were so prolific, critics say, that there were enough to build a ship. (This was disputed in the last century by a Frenchman who measured as many pieces as he could find and reported they totalled only 4,000,000 cubic millimeters; the cross on which Jesus was crucified, he argued, probably contained as many as 178,000,000 cubic millimeters.)

Three European churches had the single lance which had pierced Christ's side. At least one church, in Germany, had a vial of the Precious Blood and another possessed the Holy Cup. In the twelfth century, the emperor's palace at Constantinople had almost a complete set of "relics" of the Passion. In addition to a cross, nails, crown of thorns, and lance, there was a sponge and hyssop reed,[15] together with burial linens and a pair of Jesus' sandals.

In the previous chapter we chronicled the numerous Edessan Images and/ or Veronica's Veils, which proliferated into the Middle Ages and beyond. Although the earliest of these was reputed to have been a gift bestowed by Jesus upon King Abgar of Edessa, many of the cloths were attributed to Christ's Passion—impressed with his bloody sweat either during his agony in the Garden of Gethsemane or as he struggled with his cross on the way to Golgotha.

Of all the relics associated with Jesus' burial—including bits of the angel's candle which lit his tomb and the marble slab on which his body was laid, complete with traces of his mother's tears—most were burial linens. Although there is not the slightest hint in the gospels or anywhere else in the New Testament that Christ's burial *othonia* were preserved, certain apocryphal texts later claimed otherwise. The apocryphal writers made many such additions. For example, some found it odd that after Christ's resurrection he appeared to some of his disciples but not to his mother. "Therefore," says Marcello Craveri in *The Life of Jesus,* "certain apocryphal texts (*Acts of Thaddeus, Pseudo-Justin,* etc.) remedied this serious oversight of the canonical Gospels."[16]

Hence, in the now-lost second-century *Gospel According to the Hebrews* (in a fragment quoted by St. Jerome) it was said that Jesus himself had presented his *sindon* to the "servant [puero] of the priest." Some thought *puero* an error for *Petro* and supposed Peter had received the cloth.[17] A fourth-century account mentioned a tradition that Peter had kept the *sudarium,* although what had subsequently become of it was unknown. The narrator (St. Nino) alleged that the burial linen had been obtained by none other than Pilate's wife. This then passed to Luke, who supposedly hid it away—while neglecting to mention the fact in his gospel. Another account (about 570) averred the *sudarium* was in a cave convent on the Jordan River, even though the anonymous chronicler had not himself viewed it.

Roughly a century later a French bishop, Arculph, reported seeing a shroud of Jesus on the island of Iona (off the coast of Scotland). Arculph related a tale of how this shroud had been stolen by a converted Jew, later passed into the hands of infidel Jews, and was claimed by Christians—with an Arab ruler judging the dispute. The ruler placed the shroud in a fire from which it rose into the air, unscathed, and fell at the feet of the Christians, who placed it in a church. This shroud, said the credulous Arculph, was "about eight feet long."

Another eight-foot shroud surfaced in 877. It was presented by Charles the Bald to the St. Cornelius Abbey in Compiegne, where it was venerated for nine centuries before being destroyed during the French Revolution. Unlike this shroud of Compiegne, a rival shroud—taken as crusaders' booty from Antioch in 1098 to Cadouin, France—survived the Revolution, only to be proven a fake in 1935. The shroud of Cadouin, it turned out, was of eleventh-century Moslem origin.

Also from the eleventh century, among the relics kept at the emperor's palace in Constantinople, were listed the burial clothes of Christ—described in 1201 as still fragrant with the myrrh used in the anointing. These were said to have been "of linen, of cheap material, such as was available." Their apparently excellent state of preservation was explained: "they have defied decay because they enveloped the ineffable, naked, myrrh-covered corpse after the Passion."[18]

Thus far, in the almost twelve-century history of reputed burial garments, not one had ever been described as bearing any image. Yet, in 1204, a French Crusader named Robert de Clari wrote of the church of Saint Mary of Blachernae, in Constantinople:

...where was kept the *sydoine* [sic] in which Our Lord had been wrapped, which stood up straight every Friday so that the features of Our Lord could be plainly seen there. And no one, either Greek or French, ever knew what became of this *sydoine* after the city was taken.[19]

Although Vignon and Wilson[20] understand Robert to be describing a shroud with a body imprint, an authority on his text, E. H. McNeal, states:

Robert seems to have confused the *sudarium* (the sweat cloth or napkin, the True Image of St. Veronica) with the *sindon* (the grave cloth in which the body of Jesus was wrapped for entombment). Both relics were in the church of the Blessed Virgin in the Great Palace, and not in the church in the palace of Blachernae, as Robert says.

(McNeal cites another instance of confusion between the *sudarium* and *sindon,* a confusion that seems to have been common.)[21]

Regarding the image on the cloth, Robert de Clari's word translated above as "features" is the Old French "figure"; whether it then carried the modern connotation of "face" may be debated. So may the question of whether Robert himself had seen the cloth. Wilson argues that he did. But Humber seems nearer the truth when he notes that, since Robert arrived with the Crusaders, "it would seem that he did not see the relic with his own eyes."[22] Humber's view gains support from McNeal's comments. In any case, the Crusader could not say what became of the cloth; but we know that pieces of what was allegedly the holy shroud were distributed throughout Germany and France. One "portion" was retained for a time at Constantinople before passing in 1247 to the King of France, who then divided it into still smaller parts to be exchanged for other relics.[23]

But what is interesting about the passage from Robert de Clari is that it could have been interpreted by a later French artist as indicating a shroud bearing an imprint (not necessarily a double imprint) of Christ's body. However, the putative artist of Lirey might have gotten the idea of producing an imaged double-length shroud from other sources—including artistic ones.

A source for the double-length (though non-imaged) shroud comes from artistic scenes of the Deposition and Lamentation. Whereas earlier depictions of Christ's burial had shown a mummy-style method of wrapping the body, by the eleventh century artists began to represent the use of a double-length linen cloth, not unlike the shroud of Turin. A number of these Deposition and Lamentation examples survive from the eleventh and twelfth centuries, and several include a new motif which again anticipates the shroud: Jesus' hands are crossed rather awkwardly—the right over the left— covering the loins. This crossed-hands motif was common from the eleventh to fifteenth centuries, and at least one twelfth-century manuscript illustration shows a totally nude Christ in this pose.[24] (According to Sox, the crossed-hands pose on the shroud of Turin "looks suspiciously like a concession to medieval prudery. In Jewish burial practices, the hands are always crossed on the chest, leaving the genitals exposed."[25])

An imaged shroud might have been suggested by a source we are familiar with. From the twelfth and thirteenth centuries came exaggerated accounts of the so-called "True Image," in which it was said that Christ had imprinted the length of his body on white linen cloth. Now, the Veronica's Veil was sometimes termed the *sudarium* (as in at least two references in the twelfth century[26]), the same word used by John to describe the cloth which covered Jesus' face in the tomb; we have already seen that the burial *sudarium* was sometimes confused with the *sindon*.

Another source that may have inspired the creation of an image-bearing shroud consisted of liturgical cloths, termed *epitaphioi,* which were symbolic shrouds. From the thirteenth century (the century before the shroud of Turin's first known appearance), we begin to find these ceremonial shrouds bearing full-length embroidered images of Christ's body in the now-conventional crossed-hands pose.[27]

Thus, by this time, two traditions—represented by blank, double-length linen "shrouds" on the one hand, and whole-figured non-shroud linen cloths on the other—had been merged into a single concept: a whole-figured double-length shroud. All that remained for a fourteenth century artist/forger to do was to take the next logical step: that is, to create a "real" shroud with both a front and back image of Christ's body. Following the Veronica tradition, such a "twofold image" would be monochromatic.

In 1350 (a few years prior to the shroud's sudden appearance at Lirey), thousands of pilgrims had been attracted to an exhibition in Rome of the Holy Veronica. And, Wilson says, "Artists now showed copious bleeding in their renderings of the crucifixion where previously depiction of Christ's blood was restrained or absent altogether." Furthermore, he states:

> Mystics...attracted much attention by their lurid and graphic visions of how Christ died, a popular preoccupation intensified by the fact that at this time the Black Death was sweeping Europe. The climate was therefore exactly right for the appearance of such a macabrely detailed relic of the Passion as the Shroud.[28]

We have seen that the shroud of Turin is not consistent with the gospel narratives or with Jewish burial practices. But it does have a logical place in artistic tradition and in the climate of spurious relics. Considering the weave and condition of the cloth, the lack of provenance of the "relic" before the mid-fourteenth century, and Bishop d'Arcis' report that the cloth was "cunningly painted" by an artist who confessed the fact, the historical evidence argues strongly against the shroud being other than what Pope Clement VII judged it to be: a mere artistic "representation" of the Passion.

# 6

# Post-mortem at Calvary?

*This is the body of a well-developed male, approximately six feet tall.* So might a sindonological "post-mortem" on the man of the shroud begin. For many years, at the forefront of the pro-authenticity arguments were those relying on so-called "medical evidence," namely that the shroud image was so anatomically accurate and the "wounds" so realistic and so consistent with the pathology of scourging and crucifixion that the imprints could only be those of an actual victim of death by crucifixion.

Paul Vignon and Yves Delage, early shroud advocates in France, offered several of the arguments, which were based on perceived anatomical details, the supposed realism of the "blood flows," and so forth. But it remained for a French Catholic named Pierre Barbet, the so-called "doctor at Calvary," to address more fully the very real problems—some would say the impossibility—of authenticating the shroud from a pathologist's point of view.

Barbet, a surgeon at St. Joseph's Hospital in Paris, was approached by a clergyman friend in 1931 with a set of the Enrie photographs taken that year, and he was immediately interested. He saw the shroud at the 1933 exhibition, where he fell on his knees in devotion.[1] By then he had begun a series of grisly crucifixion experiments; for example, he obtained amputated arms and drove spikes through the hands and wrists.

Barbet published several pamphlets over the years, and in 1950 he published *La Passion de N.-S. Jesus Christ selon le Chirurgien,* translated into English in 1953 with the title, *A Doctor at Calvary.* Barbet was followed by others, including Professor Hermann Moedder, a German radiologist, who experimented with his students by suspending them from crosses and studying their reactions. An Italian contemporary of Moedder, Dr. Giovanni Judica-Cordiglia of the University of Milan, tried to explain how the bloodstains on the shroud had transferred so neatly from "body" to cloth. And in the 1960s the late Dr. David Willis, an English general practitioner, followed in Barbet's footsteps.[2]

All these men were religious defenders of the shroud. There *were* medical men who thought the shroud a fake (as for example, the Turkish doctor, Muitz Eskenazi, who delivered a paper *in absentia* at the 1950 sindonological congress in Rome[3]). However their views have been almost entirely ignored in the multitude of generally pro-authenticity articles and books.

As to Barbet, although he claimed to "remain open to any new discovery which may show me to have been wrong,"[4] the facts speak otherwise. When Dr. Anthony Sava, a long-time member of the Executive Council of the Holy Shroud Guild, obtained "very contradictory findings as opposed to those of Barbet" (by experimenting on cadavers with much fresher tissues), the French surgeon invited him to his Paris home for a discussion. Recalls Sava:

> To my utter amazement he asked me not to publish any of my findings because "they were absolutely wrong. Besides, my findings were proven correct by the very wide acceptance by the experts!" He explained further that he had done his experimental work more than twenty years before and he was no longer young and therefore unable to become involved in any revival of controversy. In all kindness to Dr. Barbet, I confess that such an attitude is far from scientific. As I saw it then and still do, truth in such matters is not determined by the degree of public approval nor by the longevity of a belief that unfortunately has a way of becoming enshrined, arbitrary and dogmatic.[5]

Sava also concluded that Barbet's "personal piety clouded the boundary between subjectivity and scientific medical appraisal."[6]

In addition to Sava the following present-day pathologists have studied the shroud:

• Dr. Robert Bucklin, deputy medical examiner for Los Angeles County, who—like Sava—is on the executive council of the Holy Shroud Guild. Also a member of the Shroud of Turin Research Project (STURP), he is something of a shroud guru to younger sindonologists and even, says *Harper's* "resembles uncannily (some say deliberately) what STURP scientists call 'the man of the shroud.' "[7] Bucklin is the best known of the pathologists who have studied the shroud image, since, in addition to his own writings,[8] he has been featured on TV shows and in several magazine articles.[9] Once himself briefly suspended on a cross in an Illinois monastery,[10] Bucklin generally follows Barbet in his arguments.

• Dr. Joseph M. Gambescia, chairman of medicine at St. Agnes Medical Center in Philadelphia. Like Bucklin a member of STURP, Gambescia also generally holds the "classical" (that is, Barbet) views.[11]

• Dr. Frederick T. Zugibe, medical examiner of Rockland County, New York. Zugibe had believed himself a member of STURP until he discovered his name omitted from a list of STURP members in a magazine article. "He now suspects," according to *Medical World News*, "that his contrary views have made him persona non grata to the STURP team and the Holy Shroud Guild." Zugibe has lamented about one sindonological meeting: "Why was everybody...all pro? Why was nobody against? I asked them, 'What is the Church afraid of? That somebody will prove it's a fake?' I thought I had gotten through to them, but I guess I was wrong."[12]

• Dr. Michael M. Baden, deputy chief medical examiner of New York for Suffolk County. Baden's views were sought by *Medical World News* because "all the physicians who so far have made pronouncements about the Shroud of Turin have necessarily been self-selected—and to some extent involved in the politics as well as the science of the mystery."[13] A distinguished pathologist, Baden brings a new objectivity—not to mention a good deal of common sense—to the question of the shroud's authenticity.

From Barbet to Bucklin, specific arguments have been offered concerning the flagellation marks, "blood flows," cause of death, and so on; these are discussed individually below.

## The Flagellation Marks

Covering the ventral and dorsal images on the shroud (more so on the dorsal) are numerous small markings which sindonologists equate with the Roman *flagrum*—a whiplike instrument for flogging, which had multiple thongs tipped with dumbbell-shaped pieces of lead or bone.[14] Barbet counted some 120 flagellation marks. Believing he could see evidence of a tendency for the marks to be paired, he guessed that the *flagrum* had two thongs; therefore, he calculated that the man of the shroud had received approximately sixty lashes.[15]

Father Rinaldi[16] counted about 125 marks, "nearly always in clusters of twos or threes," which "enable us to infer that the Condemned was scourged with little or no regard to the traditional forty legal strokes...." Forty lashes represent the limit imposed by Mosaic Law (Deut. 25:3), although to insure that the legal limit was not exceeded, only thirty-nine were actually administered (2 Cor. 11:24). But as Wuenschel argued, "With the Romans, however, the executioners were free to administer as many strokes as they pleased."[17] Monsignor Giulio Ricci, an authenticity advocate, in "Historical, Medical and Physical Study of the Holy Shroud,"[18] seems astonished that "the Romans must have been far less pitiful and more expert than the Jews if they were able to leave the victim alive in spite of the large number of lashes."

What Wuenschel terms "at first sight a discrepancy,"[19] is the fact that such a heavy scourging with a bone- or metal-tipped *flagrum* should produce wounds with so "very little blood" showing on the shroud. But Wuenschel rationalizes that when Christ was again clothed after the scourging "much of the blood must have been absorbed by the garments."

Sindonologists are able to find "evidence" on the shroud that often eludes other investigators. Yet they are often quite " positive" in what they see (*positive* being defined by Ambrose Bierce as "mistaken at the top of one's voice"[20]). Ricci, for example, says that certain "blood" trickles on the image "confirm" that the body was "bent over during flagellation."[21] Yet Barbet cites other supposed evidence "which proves that Jesus was bound with His face to the column, with His hands above Him...."[22] (Barbet's "column" to which Jesus was bound is not mentioned in the gospels; yet the flagellation of Christ was frequently portrayed by medieval artists, and the column "is a frequent iconographical subject" in their paintings.[23])

Sindonologists have persistently claimed that the marks of the *flagrum* represent a detail a medieval forger could not have known. In fact, accounts of Christian martyrdoms often mention the *flagrum*. Moreover, a sect of fanatics known as flagellants were active during the mid-fourteenth century and paintings from that period show the *flagrum*.[24] It appears to have been a commonplace. The flagellants' iron-tipped *flagra* produced sufficient blood so that Christian onlookers "dipped cloths in the flagellants' blood, which they pressed to their eyes and preserved as relics."[25]

As to the imprints of the scourge marks, Dr. Baden states emphatically that "scourge marks wouldn't leave any imprint on the shroud."[26] (His proofs are treated more fully in the text below. Can the sindonologists disprove this by demonstrating that the *flagrum* can leave clearly defined markings upon the resilient flesh of a body that will then somehow imprint with clarity on cloth? They have never done so, presumably because they cannot.

## The Crown of Thorns

The "blood" markings at the top of the head suggest that a crown of plaited thorn branches, like that mentioned in three of the four gospels (but omitted from Luke), had been placed on the man of the shroud sometime before death. Barbet and others[27] believe the array of stains indicates a "cap" or "bonnet" (covering even the top of the head), rather than a circlet.

One sindonologist, Ricci, terms this speculation a "fact" despite the very real fact that there is no imprint of the top of the head—which would be needed to confirm the notion. (This "blank space" between the otherwise head-to-head imprints argues for forgery, as Dr. Mueller observes in Chapter 8.) Ricci goes on to say:

In the Western world we think of a crown as a circular band, like a wreath. But this was not true in the Orient. In the Orient, they always used a miter, a cap—a complete cap—which enclosed the entire skull, when crowning a king. And so the fact that the marks on the skull indicate a cap, rather than a wreath, was used is not only a deviation from the traditional depiction of the crown of thorns, which is evidence of authenticity. But it is also in line with what would have been done in the East, where Jesus' shroud would have come from.[28]

But since there is no conclusive evidence that a "cap" was employed, this seems but another instance of sindonologists attempting to discover some detail a medieval artist might not have known. In fact, however, there *are* examples in Christian art, before the fourteenth century, of the "cap" of thorns.[29]

What is telling is the depiction of the "blood" flows from the "scalp wounds." Dr. Baden finds these even "more difficult to accept" than the flagellation markings. He observes, "When the scalp bleeds, it doesn't flow in rivulets; the blood mats on the hair." Dr. Baden showed a writer from *Medical World News* the body of a young woman with a head wound. Instead of neat artistic rivulets like those on the shroud—with some seeming to be almost levitated on the outside of the locks—the woman's hair was matted and caked with blood. "To me, this makes the image less real," Baden said. "It's all too good to be true. I'd expect to see a pool of blood. Whatever did this doesn't speak for severe scalp lacerations." (Indeed, it has been noted that some of the "puncture wounds" seem actually "to lie outside the outline of the scalp."[30])

## The Wounds of the Hands

Explicit mention of the nail wounds in Christ's hands is made only in John's gospel (20:25–27), with reference to doubting Thomas after the resurrection, and the word *hands* is used twice. (Less directly, Luke 24:40 states that "he showed them his hands and his feet.")

Virtually all sindonologists claim, however, that the wounds of the man of the shroud are in the *wrists.* They follow Barbet, whose experiments supposedly showed that the weight of the body dragging on the hands would cause them to tear completely free of the nails. They argue that the nails therefore pierced the wrists at what anatomists call the Space of Destot; and they further argue that this concept does not necessarily contradict John (and Luke), since the word for *hand* was often used to include the arm as well.[31]

But we must point out that since one hand is folded over the other, only one "wound" is visible and this is an exit wound. The location of this single wound has often been determined somewhat subjectively. Dr. Sava contends that "the Shroud Image does not pinpoint the very spot through which the nail passed."[32]

Sava conducted experiments that showed "that a nail introduced in the area heretofore defended by writers [the Space of Destot] could offer no greater security against tearing away than the transfixion through the middle of the palm." Sava's own conclusion (not accepted by Barbet) is that the nail instead "passed through the space between the lower ends of the radius and the ulna"—that is, "at a very short distance above the line of the wrist joint."[33]

In this regard, shroud writers often cite the discovery of the remains of an apparently first-century crucifixion victim found near Jerusalem in 1968 and known from an inscription outside the tomb as Jehohanan. The bones of Jehohanan's left arm had deteriorated too badly to be studied successfully; however the right radius was relatively intact and archaeologists found evidence at the lower end for what they believed was a scratch—possibly indicating a nail had penetrated between the radius and the ulna (as per Dr. Sava's suggestion regarding the "wound" on the shroud). But this evidence is not conclusive and represents but a single, isolated example. Moreover, those who would equate the supposed evidence from Jehohanan with the "nail wound" of the "man of the shroud" must face the fact that there were differences in other respects—particularly the different manner of nailing the feet.[34]

Furthermore, the arguments of Barbet, Sava, and others that nailing through the hands could not support the weight of the body is cast into doubt by Marcello Craveri, who states in *The Life of Jesus:*

> According to Roman practice, a stout peg was inserted between the victim's thighs and nailed to the upright so that the body would be supported and its weight would not tear the hands, which were nailed to the cross....the suppedaneum, the support for the feet that is shown in paintings and sculptures of the Crucifixion, however, did not exist.[35]

Whatever the facts may be, what is at issue is not how Jesus was crucified, nor what may be supposed about crucifixion customs from the sole example of Jehohanan. (We leave to theologians any argument derived from the presence of stigmata in saints' hands, where they were invariably located.) Instead, what concerns us chiefly is the evidence provided by the image on the shroud—specifically where the single wound is located and whether this could be consistent with a fourteenth-century artist's knowledge —an artist whose handiwork is supposedly denied by locating the nail wound in the wrist. Several things need to be said in this regard.

One concerns our earlier observation that the wound is an exit wound. Surely it is conceivable that a medieval artist could have intended to suggest that the nail had entered the upper part of the palm at an oblique angle (slanting towards the arm), thus emerging at the wrist.

In any case there is the fact that there are early artistic representations showing the wound in the wrist. Barbet speaks of "a number of exceptions" to the artistic custom of representing the wounds in the palms. On a European tour of many ancient churches STURP's husband-and-wife team, Donald and Joan Janney, reportedy "found 'several' with crucifixes dating from the middle ages in which the nails *distinctly penetrate the wrist,* not the palms."[36]

But is the "wound" on the shroud actually located in the wrist? I suggested earlier that that claim is often made on rather subjective grounds; and not all observers have agreed with Barbet et al. In the 1389 memorandum which all too briefly describes the shroud, Bishop d'Arcis merely referred to the imprints of "the wounds which He bore," without indicating anything out of the ordinary concerning the location. In the report on the shroud by the nuns of Poor Clare of Chambéry (following their repairs of the damage resulting from the 1532 fire), they specifically, according to Vignon, "mention the trickles of blood on the forearms and the marks of the nails in the *middle* of the hand. The narrator must have made a mistake here."[37]

Be that as it may, where on the shroud figure is Sava's "line of the wrist joint"? If it is where the hand tapers to its narrowest point at its intersection with the forearm, then (while the "blood flow" does extend to the wrist and forearm) the lower portion of the wound image—the rounded portion which seems to be the "exit wound" itself—is well below that line of intersection and therefore is in the base of the palm.

Moreover, writing in the French journal *L'Histoire,* Marcel Blanc reported his own study of the wound based on the Enrie photographs. His calculations definitely placed the location in the palm rather than the wrist.[38]

Dr. Zugibe agrees and explains:

> When a nail is driven through the thenar fissure of the palm, it exits between the base of the metacarpal bones of the index and second fingers and the two corresponding carpal bones at a point corresponding to the imprint on the shroud.[39]

At this location, he notes, the hand will not tear free. Dr. Zugibe reports he has established this by experiment—driving nails through cadaver hands.

## The "Missing Thumbs"

Surprising to many sindonologists is the observation that the thumbs do not show on the shroud image. Barbet sought to explain this by postulating that the nail (being supposedly driven into the Space of Destot) had caused "mechanical stimulation" of the median nerve, causing the thumb to contract toward the palm.[40] However a computer-enhanced photograph of the hands—produced by STURP's Eric Jumper, John Jackson, and Don Devan—exhibits a tiny squiggle they believe may be a faint imprint of the thumb of the uppermost hand.[41] They note that if they are correct, this casts doubt on Barbet's speculation that the thumb was contracted.

Another plausible explanation for the missing thumbs—*if* we consider the shroud as the work of an artist—is that he simply envisioned the hands folded with the thumbs underneath.

### Position and Nailing of the Feet

The ventral image is progressively indistinct from the knees downward, but from the dorsal image we can see, with relative clarity, the "bloodstained" imprint of the left foot. Barbet believed the left foot had been crossed over the right[42] but this view is doubted by the distinguished iconographer, Erwin Panofsky, who refers to the "notorious 'Holy Shroud' of Turin." According to him, "it is, to say the least, extremely doubtful that the Turin Shroud shows, or showed, the Saviour with His feet crossed." Panofsky notes that one writer had attempted to "account for the emergence of the 'three-nail-type' " of crucifixion depiction by equating the Turin cloth with the Besançon "shroud," allegedly "given to Besançon Cathedral in 1206 after having been abstracted from Constantinople in 1204." But Panofsky details what he believes are "some insurmountable objections," dismissing the alleged Constantinople-to-Besançon transfer as pious legend and observing there is "no proof" that the Besançon cloth existed prior to 1523. (Wilson agrees, terming the Besançon shroud, which was destroyed during the French Revolution, "a mere sixteenth-century copy of that of Turin."[43])

Furthermore, Panofsky observes "that all the old and independent representations of the Turin as well as the Besançon shrouds...show Christ with His legs parallel and His feet well separated." He continues:

> So far as I know, the only Shroud to show Him with His feet crossed is the late specimen at Enxobregas near Lisbon, manifestly influenced by the then generally accepted type of crucifix.

Moreover, he asks,

> ...had the "three-nail-type" been evolved from what was held to be the direct imprint of the Saviour's own body, how would it have been possible for so orthodox and well-informed a prelate as Bishop Luke of Tuy to condemn it as a wanton and irreverent innovation?[44]

If one is to disagree with Panofsky and argue that the shroud does suggest a crossed-feet position (I agree that it seems to, since the left foot points inward), then one is faced with the fact that the earliest Christian art consistently depicted the feet as nailed separately, side by side. The crossed-feet, "three-nail-type" was indeed an "innovation," although it was well-known in Europe long before the shroud first appeared at Lirey and was conventional in the West by the fourteenth century.[45]

As to the position of the "wounds" in the feet, Barbet thought there was evidence of a single nail wound (although there is an additional wound-like spot and "blood flow" from the heel). He believed this single wound suggested a nail had passed through the fleshy spot between the second and third metatarsal. Interestingly, medieval artists often placed it in such a position, just as it seems to be on the Turin Shroud.[46]

Certainly the "man of the shroud" did not have his feet nailed in the manner of Jehohanan — the sole archaeological example of an actual crucifixion. Wilson states:

> To hang him on the cross Jehohanan's executioners viciously bent his legs, forcing him into a sort of sidesaddle position and then driving the nail in from the side straight through the heel bones.[47]

Concerning the "bloodstained" right footprint, this presents a considerable challenge to authenticity that is difficult to overcome. The reader may best understand the problem by looking at the photographs of the shroud (both positive and negative) and then trying a simple experiment: lie on your back and place your right foot completely flat (as it would need to be if it were coated with blood and were to leave a footprint on cloth underneath). What one immediately notices is that, in order to place the foot flat, one must bend the knee at a considerable angle, thus raising the calf of the leg a significant distance away from the underlying cloth. Yet the calf of the right leg has imprinted.

Vignon looked at the problem another way: He conceived of the body reclining in the more natural position, with the foot resting on the back of the heel and the toes pointing upward. But "unexplained," he said, was this question: "How have the soles of the feet, and particularly of the right foot, made an impression though they are so distant from the horizontal plane?" He says,

> There are many possible reasons for this — rolls of linen may have been placed under the cloth to support the feet, the lower cloth may have been turned up to cover the feet. It is impossible to say with any certainty.[48]

Vignon has continually imagined "rolls of cloth" in various places to account for embarrassing problems posed by the imprints. As to his suggestion that the lower end of the shroud was "turned up to cover the feet," even if we suppose this *were* done, it is still difficult to reconcile with the supposed imprints on the cloth: To remain in place the end of the cloth would almost surely have to be folded well over the top of the foot with the result that there would be the added imprint of the tops of the toes and top of the foot. (In addition the ventral image would be abruptly terminated by this flap of cloth.)

## The Lance Wound

The positive (photo-reversed) image of the shroud reveals that the supposed "lance wound" is in the right side.[49] Only the gospel of John mentions the piercing of the side, and he does not specify which side was pierced. However, by rigid artistic convention, the wound was always portrayed as being in the right side. It is therefore interesting that the cloth—the provenance of which is unknown or nonexistent before the mid-fourteenth century—follows artistic tradition in this important detail.

But note the relatively small patch of "blood" from this "wound," rather than a copious flow covering at least the lower side of the body and the thigh. We find just such depictions in medieval paintings.[50] Apparently the artists envisioned a relatively small patch of blood because they imagined the blood spurting outward and away from the body. Often an angel is shown catching the "blood and water" (John 19:34) in a cup.[51]

Dr. Zugibe (who believes the shroud genuine) offers another explanation for the relatively small amount of blood: He—virtually alone among the sindonologists—believes the body was washed. Otherwise, he says, "There would have been blood all over the body and the shroud too. You couldn't have seen an image."

Zugibe stated that if a pathologist were to maintain otherwise in a homicide case, "I could kill him in court, from a forensic pathologist's viewpoint."[52] On the other hand, to account for the relatively small quantity of blood, Barbet wrote:

> It is certain that a large part of this blood must have dropped on the ground. That which remained and formed the two stains, both in front and behind, was merely the small amount which coagulated on the skin, to which it adhered owing to its viscous quality, and to which the clot will remain attached.[53]

Barbet, too, must be imagining blood spurting (from a corpse) away from the body so as not to appear down the side and upon the thigh, or else he must think that a forward attitude of the body would prevent a considerable amount of it from flowing down the body.

The second of the "two stains" Barbet refers to is that along the back of the figure, and it is consistent *only* with a horizontal position of the "body." Sindonologists see this as a realistic detail, as if additional blood had flowed after the body was taken down from the cross. But given the "picturelike" nature of these "blood" rivulets — comparable to some in medieval paintings[54] — this seems only to represent a clever touch added by a shrewd artist anxious to impart "realism." (The "blood flows" will be discussed in more detail presently.)

There does seem to be a watery "aura" at the outer edges of the "blood flow" from the side "wound," which Barbet has explained as pericardial fluid[55] — that is, fluid from the pericardium, the thin, membranous sac enclosing the heart — while Sava and others[56] are just as certain it was fluid from the chest cavity and enveloping the lungs. But there are similar "auras" around some other "blood flows" on the figure;[57] and, while these latter ones are held to be the result of the separation of clot and serum, it may be there is a single explanation for all the "auras" — namely, the medium of paint. (The chemical tests of the "blood" — which are quite damning — will be detailed in a later chapter. However, I note that in transferring blood to cloth, I did not obtain "auras" like those on the shroud, but I was able to simulate them with artists' tempera paint.)

As to the "lance wound" itself, Ricci, for one, thinks he can discern it clearly.[58] But Dr. Baden sees only "an area of darkening. I can't see any discrete injury on the chest."[59]

## "Blood" Flows

Of the "blood flows" on the shroud — some already briefly discussed — those on the arms, supposedly flowing from the pierced hands, have been the subject of much speculation. Barbet, eager to proclaim the shroud authentic, was disturbed by the stains on the arms, which ran in various directions — seemingly inconsistent with the effects of gravity. Finally he hit upon a solution. As Humber summarizes it:

> When the wrists were nailed to the crossbeams, the arms were outstretched at a ninety-degree angle to the vertical post of the cross. As soon as these nails were in place, the executioners removed their support of the body and, hanging only from the wrist nails, it sagged, causing the arms to drop from their perpendicular angle to one of sixty-five degrees. It was in this position that the blood flowed from the wrist toward the elbow in a more-or-less linear path; and since the blood flow appears primarily in this direction, it would seem that this was the predominant position of the body on the cross. However, some trickles of blood also flowed at angles of between sixty-eight and seventy degrees, indicating that the body had raised itself slightly from time to time, thus moving the arms back toward their original horizontal position.[60]

Unfortunately other angles are easily obtainable. Wilson, for example, gives measurements of 65 degrees and again of 55 degrees; the latter differs considerably from Barbet. However, none of this means much since there is no data on the angle of the arms of crucifixion victims. Various angles are represented in medieval paintings, and artists' paintings of the crucifixion of Jesus sometimes showed blood flowing from the hand wounds, running along the forearms, and dripping downward from various points along the flow.[61]

The "blood" stains on the shroud are suspiciously still red ("carmine-mauve" is a frequent description[62]), whereas aged blood turns black.[63] In addition they are "picturelike"—consistent with those in artists' paintings but unlike the transfer of real blood to cloth. This is despite enthusiastic sindonological claims to the contrary. As Robert Wilcox states:

> How the blood stained the cloth of the shroud was clearly a mystery. Paul Vignon and Pierre Barbet found, after many attempts, that it was impossible to transfer blood to a linen cloth with anything like the precision shown on the shroud. If the blood were too wet when it came into contact with the cloth, it would spangle or run in all directions along the threads. If it were not wet enough, it would leave only a smudge. The perfect-bordered, picturelike clots on the shroud, it seemed, could not be reproduced by staining.[64]

Moreover, other questions arise: How could some of the "clots" or "flows" which had *dried* (for example, those on the arms) have transferred to the cloth at all? As to blood flowing onto the cloth after the body was supposedly wrapped in it (witness the "blood" across the back which was said to have flowed onto the cloth, extending to either side of the imprint), how could such *wet* blood have dried without causing the cloth to adhere to the body? And if such blood had not dried, how could it fail to smear when the body was removed? These questions have never been satisfactorily answered.

Dr. Baden finds the picturelike "blood" markings on the shroud incompatible with reality. As Rex Rhein of *Medical World News* reports:

> To demonstrate, he [Dr. Baden] went into the morgue next to his office at Queens General Hospital and noted the complete lack of blood stains—much less well-defined wound images—on shrouds covering persons who'd met violent deaths, even though they had many cuts and open wounds. He was not prepared to accept Dr. Zugibe's explanation of a freshly washed or sweat-soaked body acting much differently.[65]

## Rigor Mortis

Referring to "facts" about the image on the shroud that "reveal that Jesus was dead," Stevenson and Habermas assert that

...his body is in a state of rigor mortis. Bucklin notes that the body is very definitely stiff and rigid. Also, the left leg has been drawn back up into the position it occupied during crucifixion, being affixed there by rigor mortis. Another example is that Jesus' head is definitely bent forward in a position fixed by rigor mortis.[66]

Father Rinaldi states: "Medical men who examine this photograph [of the shroud] detect in it the perfect characteristics of a corpse, above all that of *rigor mortis.*"[67] But *Medical World News* reported: "Dr. Baden...disagreed that Drs. Bucklin, Zugibe, or anyone else could see rigor mortis from the shroud image. 'One cannot look at pictures of a body and detect rigor mortis,' he said."[68]

Asked to respond, Dr. Bucklin admitted, "I totally agree with Dr. Baden that one can't see rigor mortis per se." Still Bucklin insisted, "But you can see *postural changes* that are consistent with rigor."[69] (Italics added.) Can this be the same Dr. Bucklin who once said, "For a scientist to be credible, he must approach his investigation with a mind free of personal opinions. Unless he is wholly objective, his findings will be influenced by his attitudes, and will be of little value."[70]

Fourteenth-century artists could portray realistic aspects of death, including what Bucklin would surely term rigor mortis, as a look at Francesco Traini's fresco *The Triumph of Death* reveals. One body is partially skeletalized, the feet pointing inward (like those on the shroud); another has his hands folded over the loins (in the familiar attitude on the shroud); and a third is bloated, his hand rigidly uplifted, his head thrown back, and his tongue protruding. (A courtly onlooker holds his nose.) This painting dates from about the time the cloth first appeared at Lirey, about 1355.[71]

## Anatomical Anomalies

"Despite decades of efforts," boasts Rinaldi, "the opponents of the Shroud have not yet succeeded in proving a single violation of the laws of anatomy and physiology in the image of the Shroud."[72] Stevenson and Habermas are among others who speak of the "anatomical accuracy of the Shroud image."[73]

What they must mean—since even Barbet admitted the right arm is longer than the left[74]—is that almost anything can be rationalized. Barbet adds:

...above all, the right forearm is also longer than the left forearm. Furthermore, the protrusion of the great right pectoral muscle is clearly broader than that of the left. There is thus a displacement of the right elbow in the outward direction, with an apparent lengthening of the right arm and forearm. This is peculiar and would indicate considerable lack of skill in a painter of genius.[75]

Ricci mentions as "not anatomically possible" the measurement "from the lips to the wound of the left carpus" which is "excessive," and also the measurement of "the front part of the legs, that in their lower portion is excessive, reaching 51 cm. in the front imprint that is 14 cm. (5.6 inches) longer than the 14.5 inches back imprint that is not interrupted."[76]

We have earlier discussed the anatomical problem concerning the feet and legs. There are other anomalies, such as the fact that the head is disembodied—seeming "detached from the rest of the body because of the apparent absence of shoulders."[77] The locks of hair at the sides of the face appear unnatural. As Vignon noted, they

> ...seem to have been stiffened and thickened. This hair is on a level with the cheek-bones. As the body is lying on its back, these locks of hair, if they had been free, would by their natural weight have fallen back on the general mass of hair which the back impression reproduces very well. These two strands of hair then must have been separated from the rest, and when the head was bowed forward may have become coagulated with dust and sweat, though this would scarcely suffice to produce this effect. Or these two locks of hair may have rested on the lateral cushions.[78]

He also states:

> The modelling of the face calls for detailed study. Nothing here is symmetrical. If the left eyebrow is normal, the right is drawn down in the middle, rising again near the nose. The mouth and the moustache are slightly contorted, the mouth a little to the left of the facial axis, the left corner raised, the right lowered.[79]

Not surprising, sindonologists such as Vignon, Ricci, and Barbet have explanations for the anatomical anomalies: the off-center mouth and moustache are "contorted"; the placement of "cushions" or "rolls of cloth" is postulated; "tucking" of the cloth here and there is assumed.[80]

Some imperfections in the facial image are "explained" as well. States Humber:

> On the face of the Shroud Dr. Barbet found a number of excoriations, wounds in which the skin is broken. These are particularly noticeable on the right side of the face, and seem to have been caused by blows with a stick approximately 1¾ inches in diameter. The most prominent of these is below the right eye-socket, but there are others on the left cheek and on the lower lip. Barbet also detected a fractured nose.[81]

Dr. Bucklin even sees a "bruise" at the tip of the nose.[82] But Dr. Baden does not see the "excoriations," "bruises," and so forth that the sindonologists think they see. As he says, "It's all in the mind of the beholder — they can't be documented."[83]

More anomalies could be catalogued. There is the relatively flat and formless dorsal image which, however, lacks the expected pressure-point flattening of the buttocks. There is the "curious space" between the hair and either side of the face,[84] and the "blank space" between the ventral and dorsal imprints (where the top of the head should have imprinted). And there is the fact that "the fingers are incredibly and excessively long, and equal to one quarter of the total length from fingertips to elbow, whereas the fingers only measure 1/5 to 1/6 of this length in a normal individual."[85] The right side of the chin "is disfigured by a blot, doubtless accidental, which [in the positive photograph] produced the impression of a deep hollow."[86] And so on.

Rather than conclude that certain anatomical anomalies of the shroud image are indicative of an artist at work, Dr. Zugibe offers a bizarre explanation: He thinks the man of the shroud, who he is convinced is Jesus, suffered from a rare disease! Noting that the figure (1) is tall and thin, (2) has long and spidery fingers, (3) has an arm span greater than his height, (4) exhibits a long, thin face, and (5) has a distance from the groin to the sole of the feet exceeding that from the groin to the top of the head, Zugibe thinks Jesus may have been afflicted with the hereditary disease called Marfan's syndrome (discovered in 1896), which is purported to have afflicted Abraham Lincoln as well. (One cannot help but wonder—considering the long, thin figures so typical of Gothic art—if Zugibe might not "discover" Marfan's syndrome to have been widespread among the medieval populace.)[87]

What I have tried to show here is that there *are* anatomical problems as well as attempts—with varying degrees of success—to explain some of them. Authenticity advocates often boast of the shroud's "anatomical accuracy," arguing (somewhat contradictorily) that such flaws as there are only further prove the shroud's genuineness since an artist capable of forming such a remarkable image wouldn't have made such mistakes. However, in subsequent chapters I intend to show that no image-forming process—other than one employed by a clever artist—could account for such a relatively *undistorted* image.

*Ethnological Considerations*

In *The Life of Jesus,* Craveri states, "On the basis of the mesocephalic shape of the head, the man of the shroud might be classified by ethnic type, as of a Mediterranean race." But he adds that "the unusual height and other physical characteristics (broad shoulders, powerful thorax, very taut abdomen, solid musculature, etc.)" would rather indicate that "the man who was selected to leave his image on the shroud of Jesus could not have been a Palestinian."[88]

Ethnologist Carlton S. Coon, states, on the other hand:

> Whoever the individual represented may have been, he is of a physical type found in modern times among Sephardic Jews and noble Arabs. The soft parts of the nose have shrunken a bit, which is simply a sign of death. I have seen the same thing in the mummies of Egyptian pharaohs.
>     For what it is worth, that is my opinion.[89]

Dr. Coon's "opinion" has been frequently quoted, but before rushing to accept it—along with his blithe observation of a "sign of death"—we should note that this is the same Dr. Coon who once examined photos of the "Iceman" creature (a hairy Bigfoot-type, said to be a "missing link" specimen frozen in a block of ice) and opined (while cautioning that his inspection was limited to the photographs):

> The pictures and description of this specimen indicate that it is a whole corpse and not some composite or model. Further, it is that not only of a Hominid but of some kind of man, though displaying a number of most unexpected anatomical features, that will be of the utmost interest to physical anthropologists.[90]

Alas, the "Iceman" was later shown to be a rubber fake, the creation of a Disneyland model-maker.[91]

Professor Silvio Curto, an Egyptologist and member of the official Commission (who suggested the shroud may have been an artistic fake), identified the racial type of the man of the shroud as Iranian.[92] And others have suggested the image is more consistent with medieval artistic conceptions than with that of a first-century Palestinian. According to Sox:

> Some observers have pointed out that what they consider is a "forked beard" on the Shroud face places it in the iconography of the high Middle Ages. The difficulty with this one is whether we are seeing a "typical" artistic forked beard. It seems curiously off-centre, if it exists at all. Added to this subjective viewing is the oft-heard remark, "it's not authentic because the Jesus on the Shroud is an old man." More serious upholders of this view point to the youthful artistic presentations of Jesus on the cross in early Christian art. We end up in circles with many of the artistic judgments made for the image.[93]

The height of the man of the shroud has been variously estimated, due to the indistinctness in the region of the feet on the ventral image and the unusual position of the feet on the dorsal image. Lorenzo Ferri, a professor at the University of Rome who participated in the first international shroud congress (1950), and who was also a sculptor, obtained a measurement of 186 cm. or 6'2".[94]

Barbet and others determined the man of the shroud was "about six foot high," a measurement also obtained by Dr. Zugibe of the "Marfan's syndrome" speculation, who found it to be "unusual for the average Hebrew of that era."[95] Vignon and Judica-Cordiglia argued for 181 cm. (approximately 5'11"). Wilson terms even this figure "an impressive height," and Weyland states, "Even with a height of 5 feet and 11 inches, Our Lord was considerably taller than the average."[96] But Stevenson and Habermas (who accept the 5'11" figure) assert:

> When estimates of the height of the man of the Shroud were first made, some objected that he was too tall for the first-century period. However, archaeologists have recently reported that the mean height of adult males found in a first-century Jewish grave site was approximately 5'10". Our modern idea that ancient men and women were much shorter than we are today is based in part on the inaccurate observation that suits of medieval armor in today's museums reflect the height of males of that time. The truth is that most surviving suits of armor belonged to young pages and not mature knights.[97]

Be that as it may (unfortunately these authors give no source for this latter "truth"), the grave site they refer to as yielding the mean height of 5'10" was one from Giv'at ha-Mivtar; it contained a limited sample of only eleven males. (Of these, one was Jehohanan—the crucifixion victim mentioned earlier—whose height was estimated at about 5'7".[98])

As to averages of height for various races, anthropologist Alfred Louis Kroeber states:

> Except for a few groups which numerically are insignificant, there is no human race that averages less than 4 feet 11 inches (150 cm) in height for men. There is none that averages taller than 5 feet 10 inches (178 cm). This means that practically the whole range of human variability in height, from the race standpoint, falls within less than a foot. The majority of averages of populations do not differ more than 2 inches (5 cm) from the general human average of 5 feet 5 inches (165 cm).

The Mediterranean racial stature is regarded as "medium," according to Kroeber.[99]

Msgr. Giulio Ricci, a Vatican archivist and longtime sindonologist, has argued that the man of the shroud was only about 5'3"—"a normal stature," reported *Newsweek*, "for a Palestinian of Christ's era." Basing his calculations primarily on measurements of the limbs, Ricci measured the forearms at 14 inches and equated this length with a 5'3" body. But others have not accepted Ricci's calculation, and indeed he seems to have erred in the wrong direction. Unless we make the special assumption that the "bloody footprint" on the shroud is the result of the cloth being folded up against it, an assumption I have already argued against, then the right leg would necessarily have to be raised a considerable amount in order for the foot to be placed flat on the cloth. Add to this Vignon's determination that the head was "bowed forward," then the length of this S-shaped "body" would be considerably greater than when it was stretched flat.[100] In any case, no definite conclusion can be reached on the basis of height alone, because it is not impossible for a first-century Palestinian to have been 5 feet or 7 feet tall.

## Cause of Death

Pro-authenticity pathologists conclude, as Wilson says, "that the corpse had suffered death by crucifixion."[101] At that point they divide into different camps. Rinaldi states:

> Dr. Barbet assumed that the Man of the Shroud, because of his position on the cross (suspended by nails in his outstretched wrists with no other support than the nailed feet) must have died of asphyxia, slowly but literally choking to death. This he claimed, was induced by muscular spasm, progressive rigidity and fixation of the chest in inspiration.[102]

Professor Möedder, however, as a result of the suspension experiments he conducted on his students, came to a different conclusion. Again Rinaldi:

> If the feet were unsupported, each [student] lost consciousness in six to twelve minutes due to profound lowering of blood pressure. If the feet were supported (as was the case of the Crucified whose feet were nailed, possibly on a rough footrest), the experiment could be maintained much longer, though, of course, not indefinitely. Möedder noticed that the progessive exhaustion and loss of consciousness were not necessarily accompanied by an excessive difficulty in breathing or a choking feeling as might be induced by muscular spasm and rigidity of the chest. He therefore concluded that the determining cause of death is definitely the phenomenon known in medicine as orthostatic collapse, i.e., the pooling of blood in the lower parts of the body due to gravity. In crucifixion death must supervene because heart and brain receive insufficient blood.[103]

Dr. Willis favored Möedder's thesis.[104] Bucklin believes death was due to congestive heart failure. He says, "The posture of the victim, the duration of the suspension and the lack of adequate support for the body weight all serve to promote a condition of diminished respiratory capacity, resulting in cardiac failure and subsequent fluid accumulation in body cavities."[105]

Dr. Zugibe suggests: "The death certificate in this case if signed today would read somewhat as follows: cardiac and respiratory arrest due to severe pulmonary edema due to cardiogenic, traumatic, and hypovolemic shock due to crucifixion."[106] But roughly a year after this suggestion by Zugibe in *Medical World News*, he was apparently considering an addition to his hypothetical "death certificate," stating that the usual cause of death in persons with Marfan's syndrome "is rupture of the aorta." This, he says, could cause blood to accumulate in the sac around the heart, which would then flow out when the soldier's lance hit that precise target.[107]

### An Expert's Dissenting Opinion

Dr. Michael M. Baden is one of the nation's distinguished medical-legal experts. An adjunct professor of law at New York Law School, he is also a lecturer in pathology at Columbia's College of Physicians and Surgeons, and a visiting professor of pathology at Albert Einstein School of Medicine. He was chairman (1977-79) of the forensic pathology panel of the U.S. Congress' Select Committee on Assassinations, which investigated the murders of President John F. Kennedy and Dr. Martin Luther King, Jr.

After examining the photographs of the shroud (both black-and-white and full-color) for *Medical World News*, Dr. Baden stated:

> If I had to go into a courtroom, I could not say there was rigor, whether the man was alive or dead, or that this picture was a true reflection of injuries on the body. In no way do I hold myself out as an expert on the shroud, but I do know dead bodies. Human beings don't produce this kind of pattern.[108]

Reginald Rhein said in that *Medical World News* article: Dr. Baden "is convinced from what he has seen that the shroud probably never contained a corpse, and that—even if it did—a qualified pathologist could not reach the kind of conclusions being held out as 'expert medical opinion' on what it purportedly shows."[109]

# 7

# Contact Prints and Vapor "Photos"

As Secondo Pia discovered when he took the first photograph of the shroud in 1898, the image on the cloth is a "negative" — or rather, the areas, which in ordinary paintings and photos show as highlights and shadows, are generally reversed; a photographic negative reverses the tones once again to return a "positive" image (at least, one that is more artistically pleasing). This property has led enthusiastic writers to term the image a "photograph of Christ"[1] and even "the first Polaroid in Palestine."[2]

But while Stevenson and Habermas state, "The concept of negativity was unknown until the invention of photography in the nineteenth century," negative images (such as those produced by rubbings from reliefs) are actually known from ancient times.[3] Nevertheless, shroud enthusiasts speak of the image on the cloth (erroneously) as a "photographic" negative.[4] One who should know better, a British photographer and sindonoloist named Leo Valla, gushes:

> I've been involved in the invention of many complicated visual processes, and I can tell you that no one could have faked that image. No one could do it today with all the technology we have. It's a perfect negative. It has a photographic quality that is extremely precise.[5]

But as I will show in Chapter 9, Mr. Valla was too hasty in his pronouncements. In fact, while the shroud image is a quasi-negative, the analogy with photography breaks off there, since — as our photographic consultant, James R. Burke, observes — the image differs from a photographic negative in several important respects:

1. There are blank spaces surrounding the various imprinted forms (for example, nose, cheeks, etc.) within the outlines of the figure.

**2.** The beard is opposite in tone to what we should expect (dark on the original "negative" imprint), giving the effect, when a positive is made, that Jesus was a white-bearded old man.

**3.** There are certain distortions in the image (noted in the previous chapter) not characteristic of photographs.

If the image is not truly "photographic," nevertheless one wonders how such a quasi-negative image might have been formed. In this chapter we will look at two early hypotheses of image formation, both of which may be regarded as "natural," in order to distinguish them from the "supernatural" and the "artistic" (which will be discussed in the following chapters).

## The Contact Hypothesis

As Bishop d'Arcis noted in his fourteenth-century report to Pope Clement (although the bishop had learned, he stated, that the image was actually "cunningly painted"), the Lirey dean "and his accomplices" were claiming the image of Christ had been "impressed" onto the cloth. If one supposes the body were covered with some substance capable of recording an impression—burial ointments, for example, or a "bloody sweat"—then a negative imprint makes sense. That is because the pronounced areas of relief (the bridge of the nose, the cheekbones, and so forth) would produce correspondingly dark areas on the cloth, whereas in a positive photograph or painting such areas show as highlights. Similarly, the deeper recesses would not touch the cloth, and those areas would remain white (on the white cloth); whereas, again, in a positive image such areas would be dark.

Thus, at first thought, an obvious explanation for the image on the shroud would seem to be that it was the result of simple contact between a body and cloth. If this hypothesis of image formation could be successfully demonstrated experimentally, however, that still would not prove the shroud's authenticity, since an artist or forger could obviously coat a body or statue with a suitable staining medium and produce similar results. On the other hand, disproving the hypothesis would not necessarily *disprove* authenticity unless it could be shown that other hypotheses of image formation (other than artistry) could also be decisively eliminated.

The "contact hypothesis" can, in fact, be disproved on several grounds. One is that such imprints tend not to have gradations in tones (image intensity) like those of the shroud,[6] but rather are characterized by something of an either/or effect. Either an area imprints (with imprinted areas being of a similar tone) or it does not (resulting in blank space). As a consequence there is also a tendency for such prints to have abrupt or "hard" edges, whereas the image areas on the shroud (for example, the cheeks) have feathered or "soft" edges, leading to the conclusion that the image-forming process had "inherent edge-blurring properties."[7] A forger, however, might have deliberately "softened" the edges—particularly if his medium were in a powdered form, such as chalk. As Vignon noted, "If the shading of the contours is desired, rub gently with the finger when the print is finished in such a way as to gradate them, and it is done."[8]

However, unless the (hypothetical) contact print were made by an artist, ordinary handling—wrapping the body in the cloth and "tucking"[9] the latter here and there—should have resulted in badly smudged imprints, not merely gradated ones. Clearly this has not happened with the shroud.

Also arguing against contact as the image-forming process is the fact that not all the areas which have imprinted would have been touched by a cloth simply draped over a body. This problem would be especially critical in the details of the face.[10]

Yet another argument against the contact hypothesis invokes the law of gravity: Far less pressure is exerted by a lightweight cloth resting upon a body than is exerted by a body resting heavily upon a cloth placed under it. In other words, the frontal image should appear noticeably lighter than the dorsal one—*if* the two imprints resulted from simple contact. An official STURP report states, however:

> . . . the densities at presumed contact points on both frontal and dorsal images do not differ significantly. These characteristics along with the superficial nature of the image would suggest that the contact transfer mechanism is pressure-independent.

The report calls attention to this "apparent contradiction."[11]

But the strongest argument against cloth-to-body contact as the image-forming mechanism follows from the laws of geometry: When a cloth is wrapped about a three-dimensional form (coated with spices, for example) and then taken off and laid flat, the resulting image will be considerably distorted, as Vignon observed long ago. "That is why," he concluded, "we cannot hope to obtain by simple contact good reproductions of a delicate object such as the human face."[12] Vignon learned this lesson by submitting to an experiment at the Sorbonne. He recalled:

> The writer lay down on an operating-table, and his face was carefully smeared with red chalk. The same thing had been done to a false beard which was fixed on to his face in order to approach as nearly as possible to the conditions indicated on the print [the shroud]; in order also to bring all the lower part of the face to one plane.[13]

Reproducing photographs of his experimental images, which are grotesquely distorted, Vignon confessed "that we radically failed in our attempt to reproduce by a mechanical process impressions similar to those on the shroud."[14] He added: "The forger could doubtless have obtained the imprints of a body and limbs by simple contact, but he could *not* have obtained the portrait of the head; this theory must be abandoned."[15]

Before abandoning the "theory" myself, in 1977 I too conducted experiments, using my own face as a relief. When my first attempt was a hopeless failure, I modified my approach, recalling Reverend Wuenschel's assertions that new linen in that twill pattern would be "somewhat stiff" and that "from the imprint it is clear that at either side of the head there was some kind of support [Vignon's imagined "small rolls of linen"] which held the cloth practically flat."[16]

Fastening canvas fabric loosely over a frame, and coating my face with a semi-moist rouge, I made a print—a negative, which a photographer's negative in turn converted to a positive image. In many respects it was much better than Vignon's efforts and one sindonologist conceded to me privately that it was among the best of its kind. It was, however, a failure—with distorted, overly wide eye sockets, a severely fractured bridge of the nose and a flattened nasal tip, among other flaws—and I suggested[17] that a sculpted relief (a lower relief to minimize the distortions) might have been employed. That suggestion, I thought, would account for the fact that while my experimental imprint recorded the actual texture of my moustache (along with some other fine details), such texture was lacking in the portrait on the shroud. Like Vignon before me, I abandoned the contact-imprint hypothesis, and so have virtually all investigators.

But one who has not abandoned it is sindonologist Samuel Pellicori, a member of STURP who is still clinging to this straw of a disproven hypothesis. Pellicori has been experimenting on linen with such substances as olive oil and burial spices (myrrh and aloes) as well as skin secretions—for instance "a sample wiped from the back of the neck" which was "visually dirty before baking" (baking being a method of artificially simulating natural aging).[18] He has obtained stains roughly similar to those of the shroud in color—that of age-yellowed linen—which he explains as due to cellulose degradation and dehydration.[19] But what Pellicori has established, according to Dr. Mueller, is merely that "yellowing of linen due to cellulose dehydration can be caused by a large variety of common substances, perhaps nearly anything, in contact with linen."[20]

Nevertheless, on the basis of this observation, Pellicori asserted: "This strongly suggests that substances on the body once enclosed in the Shroud—either burial ointments, perspiration or skin secretions—transfigured [sic] the cloth through direct contact."[21] However, since none of these substances have been detected on the fibers of the shroud,[22] and since a forger might have used any of a number of cellulose-degrading substances,[23] Pellicori has obviously rushed to judgment in proclaiming, "The Shroud is not the product of a clever Medieval artist."[24]

It is one thing, of course, to produce random stains and blotches and quite another to create an entire negative portrait having minimal distortions. Since none of Pellicori's articles mentions his having actually *tested* the very hypothesis he was advocating—the contact hypothesis—I wondered why. I even wrote a letter to an editor in which I not only recommended Pellicori try to produce an acceptable contact imprint of a face, but also offered not to object to *any* printing medium he might choose to use (rouge or printer's ink would seem easier to work with than perspiration) nor to object to his carefully patting the cloth to obtain optimum results (although it seems unlikely a corpse would have been subjected to such unusual treatment). The letter went unpublished, but then an article in *Science 81* reported that, while Pellicori had produced a handprint,

> the same technique on his face, however, failed to turn up facial detail with the minimal amount of distortion of the original. So even if Pellicori is right [as to cellulose degradation], he has solved only one part of the mystery: His theory [actually it is only an hypothesis] may explain how the decaying cellulose in the shroud reacted with substances to form an image, but it does not explain the incredibly lifelike details, especially in the areas of the face where the cloth would not have touched the skin. Furthermore, it gives no indication of how relief information [represented by the tonal gradations] was encoded on the shroud.[25]

And so Pellicori's assertions that the shroud is not a forgery and that there had been a "body once enclosed in the Shroud"—are not only unwarranted but reveal a lack of due scientific caution and objectivity.

## Vignon's "Vaporography"

Since there are imaged areas within the outlines of the "body" imprints that would not have been touched by a simple draped cloth, Vignon concluded the image must have been "the result of action *at a distance* (that is to say without contact); geometrically speaking is a *projection*."[26] And so a pair of early sindonologists—termed "the believer and the agnostic"[27]—advanced a "theory" to explain the supposed phenomenon.

The "believer" was Paul Vignon himself, a Catholic. Thomas Humber has described him:

> Born to wealth in Lyon, France, in 1865, Vignon was able to pursue a multiplicity of interests without the burden of financial considerations. He loved to go mountain-climbing, and he vigorously pursued the sport until 1895,

when a physical and nervous breakdown brought on by his relentless challenge of the most dangerous peaks forced him to exchange his athletic prowess for more sedate, if no less challenging, pursuits.[28]

In 1900, as a "young biologist"[29] at the Sorbonne, Vignon teamed up with Yves Delage, reportedly an agnostic, a zoologist of some note. Delage was elected to the French Academy of Sciences in 1901, and continued his studies even after becoming blind in 1904.[30] In 1902, the year Vignon published *The Shroud of Christ*, Delage outraged the Academy by giving a half-hour lecture with the not-too-agnostic-sounding title, "The Image of Christ Visible on the Holy Shroud of Turin," in which he asserted the shroud was genuine. How was the image produced? "Science" had supposedly determined it was the result of "vaporography." So far-fetched was this "theory" that it is little wonder the Academy was outraged. Yet pro-shroud writers still sometimes like to say, with Humber, that critics of Delage and Vignon "reacted hysterically."[31]

With his reputation in danger and Turin authorities refusing to allow him to make a proper examination of the "relic," Delage abandoned his pseudoscientific liaison with the shroud and returned to his scientific endeavors. But Vignon, "the believer," continued his futile pursuit of the elusive vapors he believed had produced the image. (While it had been Delage who had instigated the investigation of the shroud at the Sorbonne, it was actually Vignon—apparently caught between the failure of his contact experiments and an overwhelming need to support the shroud's authenticity—who had concocted the "vaporograph theory.")

Briefly, vaporography is predicated on a physico-chemical process: Presumably body vapors interacted with spices on the cloth (likened to a sensitized photographic plate) to produce a vapor "photograph" or "vaporograph." Normal perspiration contains urea, and "morbid sweat" (produced by a body in agony) contains a much larger amount. Fermentation converts urea to ammonium carbonate, which in turn yields alkaline (ammoniacal) vapors. The Gospel of John refers to aloes as one of the burial spices used to anoint Jesus' body; and aloes mixed into a paste with olive oil yields aloetine, which turns brown in the presence of ammonia. Vignon thus believed he had a viable image-forming process.

Working with a friend, René Colson, from the Ecole Polytechnique in Paris, Vignon began experimenting. According to Humber:

Their best results were obtained by moistening a plaster cast of a hand with ammonia, inserting it into a kid glove and exposing it to a cloth soaked with aloetine. The print thus obtained showed the mass of each finger, but was graduated with such delicacy that no lines of division appeared. Experiments with larger objects, such as plaster heads, were far less successful, mainly because merely moistening plaster with ammonia produced too fast and free a flow of vapors. But it would not have been impossible to duplicate the conditions under which the Shroud's image had [supposedly] been formed, and even the moderate success of Vignon's experiments assured him that he was correct.[32]

He was, after all, a "believer."

Unfortunately, even Vignon's "best results" have come under suspicion. Eric Jumper, a member of STURP, states:

> This hand image, I must admit is now rather infamous since neither I nor anyone I have contacted has ever seen a picture of it. . . . Be that as it may, it is important to note two points. (1) A prerequisite for image formation was a damp cloth and (2) Vignon reported that his hand image was clearly visible on the back of his test cloth as well as on the front.[33]

The image on the shroud, in contrast, is confined to only the topmost fibrils.[34]

Another argument against the postulated vapor-transport mechanism (that is, vaporography) is that images so produced would tend to become "saturated"; in other words, they would reach "a certain stain intensity and not get any darker."[35] The tonally graded shroud images do not exhibit saturation.

And then there is the problem of resolution—of the clarity of the image.[36] Because vapors do not travel in straight (vertical) lines, but instead diffuse and convect, highly resolved images like those on the shroud would be virtually impossible by vaporology. In 1977 I conducted several experiments with regard to the vapor-transport mechanism, and reported:

> Even using chemicals that would produce clear reactions (one to treat the cloth, the vapors of the other coming in contact with it), a detailed image cannot be produced. I attempted to make a vaporograph of a mask, and all I got was a big round blur.[37]

That is a layman speaking. Stated in scientific terms, "a material distributed by diffusion would be essentially isotrophic ($1/r^2$ density) and susceptible to convective fluctuations, and, therefore, would not preserve the shading and resolution."[38]

As if the foregoing objections were not enough to demolish the "vaporograph theory," there is the added fact "that the amount of ammonia needed to produce a satisfactorily intense image is greater than might be expected from the natural reactions" on which vaporography is predicated.[39]

Finally, the microscopic and chemical analyses of fibrils removed from the shroud image, conducted by several laboratories, failed to detect the postulated organic substances (that is, aloes and olive oil).[40] (This is one of the same objections faced by Pellicori's hypothesis that an oil-and-spice-covered body might have produced the images on the shroud by simple contact.)

As a result of these insurmountable objections, the "vaporograph theory"—once regarded by many sindonologists as all but proven—is no longer given any credence by serious and knowledgeable investigators. In fact, a report by STURP scientists concluded: "The evidence seems to be quite conclusive for ruling out the Vignon vaporographic theory as an image formation hypothesis."[41]

But recently new Vignons have imagined a process of image formation that also fits into the category of processes acting across a distance. As we shall see in the following chapter, these believers have embraced the notion that a *miracle* occurred to produce the image

# 8

# Resurrection Radiance?

*Evolving "Theory"*

If neither simple contact nor elusive vapors were the cause of the shroud image, other mechanisms would be suggested. In a 1931 issue of *The Catholic Medical Guardian*, an English military officer named O'Gorman took aim with his own "theory." Robert Wilcox explains:

> What O'Gorman came up with was a theory combining the action of four different agents: oxidizing vapors such as those postulated by Vignon; radioactive substances which may have been in the burial spices or even in the body parts themselves; "electrical radiations of an auracal nature;" and "a sudden radiance of our Lord's body at the moment of resurrection."[1]

Vignon had been out done. With phrases like "electrical radiations of an auracal nature," sindonology was being spiffed up for its crusade into the world of modern science.

In the 1960s when the vaporograph hypothesis was gasping its last ammonia-dependent breaths — Geoffrey Ashe revived and simplified O'Gorman's hodge-podge "theory." Ashe, also British, had the notion that some mysterious type of radiation (he was necessarily vague about this) might have "scorched" the image onto the shroud. To test his "theory," Ashe heated a small metal medallion (a shallow relief of a horse), laid a handkerchief over it, and — when the "scorch picture" began to show through the cloth — quickly lifted it off. The result, says Wilcox, "was a negative picture of the

---

*Note: This chapter was co-authored by Dr. Marvin M. Mueller, a research physicist at the Los Alamos National Laboratory. See page 6 for full biographical information.*

horse that was quite detailed."[2] Actually it was little more than a crude, fuzzy silhouette—even though the relief was so low as to have been virtually flat. (Nowhere were there deep recesses and high prominences like those of a human face.) It would seem that, at best, Ashe's experiment only suggested a possible mechanism for forgery. Yet he appears to have thought he had done something truly profound in its implications.

> The physical change of the body at the resurrection may have released a brief and violent burst of some radiation other than heat—perhaps scientifically identifiable, perhaps not—which scorched the cloth. In this case, the shroud is a quasi-photograph of Christ returning to life, produced by a kind of radiance or "incandescence" partially analogous to heat in its effects . . . . In conclusion, the acceptance of the holy shroud as a "scorch picture"—whatever the precise mode of creation—justifies the following statement: "The shroud is explicable [only] if it once enwrapped a human body to which something extraordinary happened. It is not explicable otherwise."[3]

We might attribute such nonsense to Ashe's not being a scientist. Less easy to comprehend is a scientist taking it seriously. But more than one scientist did: Indeed, STURP itself was organized by a score or more scientists of sindonological bent, who treated the radiation-caused scorch hypothesis as worthy of the most serious consideration. By the time of the organizational meeting of STURP (at Albuquerque, N.M., in March 1977), most of the membership seemed convinced that the peculiar properties of the shroud image could only be consistent with a scorch somehow produced by radiation projecting across the body-to-cloth distances. Since this "theory" has never been published in the scientific literature, the *Proceedings*[4] of that meeting are still the best place to learn the reasoning and methodology behind this interpretation, as well as the general tone and motivations behind the founding of STURP.

But we are getting ahead of an interesting story concerning the founders of STURP. The seminal idea—that modern techniques of image enhancement could profitably be applied to the image on the shroud of Turin—was conceived in 1974 by John Jackson, a young Air Force physicist working with lasers at the Air Force Weapons Laboratory in Albuquerque. Jackson had had a longstanding interest in the shroud; so, when he was exposed to the powerful new techniques of digital image enhancement, their employment in analyzing and probing the ancient image seemed natural. He soon teamed up with another young Air Force captain, aeronautical engineer Eric Jumper. (Both serve on the Executive Council of the Holy Shroud Guild.)

Together, they soon decided to test Vignon's old assertion that shroud-image density (darkness) correlates inversely with cloth-to-body distance when a shroud-like cloth is draped over a suitable recumbent volunteer.[5] Whereas Vignon's claim was hardly more than a hunch based on qualitative visual observations, Jackson and Jumper, with a panoply of up-to-date instrumentation available to them, were able to quantify the correlation through experimentation. What they found was a correlation that, although imperfect (due to data scatter and measurement errors), exceeded their expectations. This information could then be used to reconstruct a full-size, three-dimensional statue of the "man in the shroud," as they called it. Needless to say, the impact of this discovery sent shock waves around the world of sindonology, and an Albuquerque conference was scheduled for March 1977.[6]

Prior to this, however, several scientists at the Los Alamos National Laboratory in northern New Mexico had joined the team, due to a chance encounter between Jackson and Robert Dinegar, an Episcopal priest as well as a physical chemist at Los Alamos, at a course in theology being given in Santa Fe. The interesting technical puzzle posed by the existence of the correlation and its interpretation as a "3-D image" paved the way for an unlikely liason between modern science and sindonology.

The puzzle existed because photographs and ordinary paintings, with light and shadow depending on the source and angle of illumination, do not exhibit the same kind of correlation (even for a nude figure of relatively constant color or reflectance). Furthermore, for completely diffuse (shadowless) illumination, the point-to-point image darkness depends solely on color or reflectance changes on the subject—not on the relief. The shroud image, exhibiting none of the usual photographic or artistic tonalities with respect to highlighting or color, is indeed unusual. But then so would be the intent of a putative artist: to depict an image somehow formed by the contact or near contact of a body with the shroud enveloping it—a process involving topographics rather than lighting.

Combined with preliminary observations indicating that the image characteristics (for example, color) were similar to those of lightly and superficially scorched linen,[7] the so-called 3-D effect resulted in the hypothesis that the image was the result of "flash photolysis" caused by a "short burst" of "radiant energy," probably emanating from the body of Christ at the moment of resurrection.[8] Judging from their statements quoted in the press and in television interviews, it appears that nearly all of the new members joining STURP at that time accepted this hypothesis as the only viable one in the light of the evidence then available.

Several of the scientists involved, both at Los Alamos and nationwide, made scientifically irresponsible statements that proclaimed the radiation-scorch hypothesis to be based on facts, even before they had examined the shroud. Three statements by physical chemist Ray Rogers of Los Alamos[9] (who later, and to his credit, took a more cautious stance) will indicate the tenor of early STURP investigations:

> I am forced to conclude that the image was formed by a burst of radiant energy—light, if you will. I think there is no question about that.
>
> What better way, if you were a deity, of regenerating faith in a skeptical age, than to leave evidence 2,000 years ago that could be defined only by the technology available in that skeptical age.
>
> The one possible alternative is that the images were created by a burst of radiant light, such as Christ might have produced at the moment of resurrection.

Similar statements from other investigators were distributed internationally by the wire services, and some even found their way into an article concerning the shroud investigation which appeared in the prestigious journal, *Science*.[10] The year 1978 was indeed a great one for sindonology.

With such statements from reputable scientists at several prominent laboratories in their hands, it is hardly surprising that the media made the most of it and, uncritically, distributed this supernatural interpretation. As commonly happens in circumstances suggesting a paranormal or supernatural explanation, the old journalistic maxim that extraordinary claims demand extraordinary examination was conveniently forgotten.

## 3-D or Not 3-D?

As to Jackson and Jumper's determination that tonal values in the shroud image were a function of cloth-to-body distance, their observed correlation is only fair. Their statement that it is "apparent that the image on the Shroud must be equivalent to a three-dimensional surface of Jesus' body"[11] is totally unwarranted, due to methodological flaws. Their methodology requires considerable explanation, however, and is treated here in four steps.

1. For their first step, a cloth bearing a tracing of the shroud image is draped over a recumbent human-male model of "proper height and proportions"—assuming the man of the shroud to have been a particular height and weight, neither of which is stated (we learn elsewhere the model was "about 5 ft. 10 in. and weighing about 176 lbs."[12]). They then adjust the cloth so that, as they say,

> ...all image features were aligned over the corresponding body parts. Under the assumption that all blood marks indicated a direct body contact point, we required that all such marks touch the subject. Care was taken to assure that all body images were over the appropriate body features though not necessarily in contact.[13]

But their published photographs and sketch[14] reveal that they did *not* place the foot of their human model upon the "blood"-stained "footprint" of the dorsal image, which would have resulted in the model's leg being considerably raised from the cloth (as we discussed in Chapter 6). In fact their overall placement of the model (fully supine) is at variance with the reconstruction (an S-shaped posture) argued for by Ian Wilson.[15] (Wilson, however, seems to contradict himself by favorably citing Jackson and Jumper's experiment, yet offering his own reconstruction with markedly different cloth-body distances.) Again, Barbara Sullivan in 1973 prepared tracings of the shroud images and attempted to account for mismatching of the ventral and dorsal imprints (noting the latter "appears slightly longer"). She concluded that the data "do seem to suggest that the image [sic] is somewhat hunched and lies to one side."[16]

Having draped this particular cloth over the particular model in a particular way, the two STURP scientists then take horizontal photographs of the model, covered with the cloth as well as uncovered, and prepare a profile drawing from the photographs. From the drawing, the vertical cloth-body distances along the ridgeline are then determined by measurement—a more error-prone technique than it appears.

2. The next step of the process requires measuring image intensity (that is, the relative variations in the tones) of the shroud images. For this, one uses a microdensitometer, an instrument that measures the amount of light transmitted (related to the optical density) through the various microscopic areas of a photographic transparency of the shroud. (Jackson and Jumper used a 1931 Enrie lantern slide of the shroud for this.) The microdensitometer tracing along the ventral ridgeline alone yields what the two scientists term "a distorted profile of Jesus' body" (given their prior assumption). Actually it is grotesque—scarcely recognizable as anything human—but it will be "corrected" in the next step.

3. Then image intensity and cloth-body distance are correlated by plotting them on a graph. The correlation is actually only fair—with considerable data scatter—but it indicates a roughly exponential fall-off (to near-zero image intensity in slightly less than two inches). The next step is to impose a more perfect correlation (than was actually obtained) by drawing a smooth curve through the region of scattered data points. But any of a number of different curves could equally be chosen to average the data scatter and replace it with a smooth function. As one STURP report stated: "Considerable uncertainty exists in the analytic form of their original function because it was chosen somewhat arbitrarily to represent the relatively impressive correlation of data over a limited region."[17]

4. Finally, the two scientists use this smooth curve, which they call the "mapping function," to correct the grotesque microdensitometer-traced pro-

file of the "man of the shroud." The resulting profile now begins to look rather human, but is still somewhat distorted; so two more corrective procedures are employed. First, the assumed geometrical drape-shape of the cloth is factored out. (We have already seen that numerous different configurations can be postulated for how the presumed body was wrapped.) Second, the mapping function is also iteratively modified so that a more human-looking figure can be obtained. The final result of all this adjusting and correcting and smoothing is—the reader has surely guessed—a three-dimensional figure that looks relatively normal. This 3-D image can be shown on a computer-generated graph[18] or, alternately, used to construct a cardboard statue of the "man of the shroud."[19] But there is one problem remaining: If the face is adjusted to show normal relief, the body appears to be in bas-relief.

The salient point in all this is that the whole methodology of three-dimensional reconstruction is dependent on circular reasoning, and begs the question of whether or not the shroud ever enveloped a real human form.[20] Furthermore, if there were no measurement errors in determining cloth-body distance, and no data scatter in the correlation plot (of image darkness versus distance), then the STURP scientists would simply wind up with a three-dimensional relief of the human model chosen for the experiment. Ironically, while the smoothing of the data scatter itself produces distortion of the reconstructed relief, it also allows some of the shroud-image characteristics to be superimposed on the relief of the human model. Hence the resultant "statue" is actually some blend of the characteristics of the shroud image and the human model—not, as has been asserted, "a three-dimensional image of the man buried in the Shroud."[21]

By their involved, questionable process, Jackson and Jumper have shown they can obtain a *fair* correlation of tonal variations in the shroud image versus corresponding cloth-to-body distances (based on an assumed body-in-cloth configuration). But—since correlation does not imply causality— that is all they have done. Some degree of internal consistency in tonal gradations over localized regions of the shroud image is all that they have established—despite five years of media hype.

Their methodology does *not* demonstrate that the shroud image was formed by any kind of projection across a distance from "body" to cloth, let alone that the image was produced by a miraculous burst of radiation and represents proof of Christ's resurrection.[22] It does not even imply that any three-dimensional form—body or statue—was ever wrapped in the cloth, and it by no means disproves human artistry as a possible category of image-forming mechanisms.[23]

And yet it is this assertion that the touted 3-D characteristics imply projection—coupled with the scorch-like color and image surface qualities— that has been cited repeatedly as evidence for some kind of radiation as the imaging process. In the following chapters we will see that other processes also exhibit these characteristics.

## Radiation Scorches

Leaving aside the question of an unprecedented source, we shall now consider the possible kinds of radiations, their transport across distance, and their interaction with cloth. Such considerations immediately invoke the unparalleled conceptual power and scope of modern physics. Let the reader be assured, however, that we shall not delve deeply into physics here, but will only list some properties of various radiations.

The two classes of radiation are electromagnetic and particle. The properties of the former vary with wavelength over a mind-boggling range from gamma rays and X-rays at the short end of the spectrum; through ultraviolet, visible, and infrared in the middle; and to microwaves and radio waves at the long end. Only those in the middle, from UV to IR, could (assuming sufficient intensity and a short temporal pulse length) scorch cloth superficially. However, as Jackson and Jumper's correlation plot shows, the scorching effect would have to fall off to near zero in a projection distance of less than two inches. No electromagnetic radiation, except for very short UV (which is strongly absorbed by air), behaves in that manner.

When we turn to particle radiations (atomic or subatomic), a similar situation obtains: All can be eliminated save for low-energy electrons and fairly-low-energy ions. However, needless to say, corpses do not emit any of these radiations. The crucial issue, besides the unprecedented source, lies in the nature of projective imaging itself, as we shall now see.

Given any source of any natural radiation, there is *no* way to projectively image it without using refractive elements (lenses of some kind) or collimating elements (pinholes or arrays of pinholes) between the source and the image surface. This is an unquestionable fact of geometry and optics for natural-radiation sources. It is much exacerbated for a postulated image as large as that on the shroud supposedly formed 0-2 inches from the source of the radiation. Here there is *no* conceptual solution, even in principle. The only possible way of forming an image under those conditions would involve an array of more than a hundred thousand properly spaced pinholes, but even this would not form an image as good as that on the shroud.

There is one last, desperate conceptual solution: Posit that, as in a laser, the radiation emitted from each element of body (and hair) surface is collimated (that is, emitted only in parallel directions, in this case vertical). Then an image would be formed, independent of distance, without the use of an array of pinholes. In effect, the body surface would be composed of millions of lasers aligned more or less vertically. In principle, the resultant image could be of much better quality than the half-centimeter resolution of the shroud image. The problem is that this conceptual solution necessarily invokes the supernatural. Then the question becomes why the shroud image is not of *better* quality than it is. But the core issue is, of course, if you posit a miracle then *any* discussion of mechanism is beside the point (until, perhaps, a physics of miracles is developed).

## Unnecessary Invocation

In light of the evidence presented thus far, as well as that to be presented in subsequent chapters, invoking the supernatural is completely unwarranted. In fact, the whole notion of a radiation "scorch picture" should have been laid to rest long ago. For one reason, scorches on linen (including those present on the shroud from the 1532 fire) exhibit strong reddish fluorescence, while the shroud images do not fluoresce at all.[24] Moreover, STURP scientists, conducting many experiments with lasers of diverse wavelengths and pulse-widths, have totally failed in their attempts to duplicate the microscopic shroud-image characteristics by lightly scorching linen.[25]

Another serious flaw in the idea of radiation scorching lies in the fact that the image coloration generally resides only in the topmost fibers of the surface threads, and does not follow the (unshadowed) dips of the threads in the weave pattern.[26] This crown-effect does not seem consistent with a projected image. Neither do some other characteristics. For example, at low magnification the imaged areas take on the appearance of a random checkerboard, with colored areas interspersed with ostensibly uncolored areas.[27] (This may be seen in a published photomicrograph.[28]) Such an effect should not result from mechanisms (radiations, vapors) acting across a distance, but has been observed by one of us [J.N.] on woven fabric which has been rubbed with substances such as pigments.

Still another strong argument against the projected-image hypothesis is based on the absence of any imaging between the otherwise head-to-head body images. Under the assumption of authenticity, this is the region in which the cloth was folded over the top of the head. Given Jackson and Jumper's correlation plot, any part of the cloth within two inches of skin or hair should show some image-type darkening. Thus, under the projected-image hypothesis, the blank space would mean that the cloth was *everywhere* two inches or more from the hair in the curved "overhead" region. Based on measurements on Enrie's shroud photo, the blank space is no more than about 6.5 inches long, and could be less than 6 inches. (There is some uncertainty in the measurement, amounting to roughly ± 0.5") This piece of data, along with the assumption that the head of the "man in the shroud" was shaped normally, leads to the conclusion that a blank space should not be there. The corollary is that the cloth could not have been arched or "tented" two inches or more from the hair on top of the head. Even under the unlikely assumptions that the "man in the shroud" was microencephalic (axial head length of five inches) and that the real blank-space distance is seven and a half inches, the air gap between cloth and hair could not have exceeded two inches except in the very centermost region at the top of the head. Hence, even under the most favorable assumptions, the blank space should be far smaller than what is observed if the image were formed by projection.

However, as we have seen, the resolution of the image demands that the postulated radiation be collimated approximately vertically at emission from the body surface. If this is assumed to apply to the hair on the top of the head as well, then one would indeed expect a blank space similar to the one on the shroud. However, the corollary is that then the hair emission would be concentrated as a band of enhanced brightness emitted (both up and down) from the top of the head. Such does not seem to be present in the shroud photos.

Given the strong evidence against radiation scorching, Ray Rogers recently lamented, "I incline toward the idea of a scorch, but I can't think how it was done. At this point," he added, "you either keep looking for the mechanism or start getting mystical."[29]

Stevenson (until recently, spokesman for STURP) and Habermas have indeed gotten mystical. As they state in their book:

> In light of the further probability that the Shroud is the actual burial garment of Jesus, it is also probable that the cause of the image corresponds to the historical report that Jesus rose from the dead....
> In other words, the resurrection of Jesus is also the best explanation for the lack of decomposition, the absence of any unwrapping of the body, and the presence of the heat or light scorch.[30]

(Elsewhere they consider—but reject—the possibility it was "a satanic ploy."[31])

In one of the most ludicrous and ill-informed articles[32] we have read about the shroud, Jerome Goldblatt thought the shroud image was produced by thermonuclear reactions and was analogous to laser-produced holograms. Needless to say, the article is out of touch with the facts (by about four years) and with reality (by some greater measure).

Completely untenable, the "radiation-scorch" hypothesis must go the way of the contact and "vaporograph" hypotheses, and so those who would argue for the shroud's authenticity are left without any viable hypothesis for the formation of the image. When that fundamental problem is added to the other evidence presented thus far—the lack of provenance, the reported confession of an artist, the suspiciously red and picturelike "blood" stains, and so on—it should be obvious that a serious consideration of possible *artistic* methods of image creation is warranted.

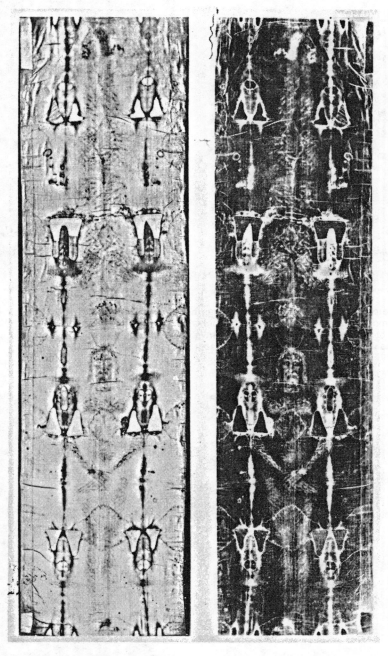

**Plate 1.** *Left:* The cloth now known as the Shroud of Turin is a piece of linen, approximately 3½′ x 14′, bearing the faint sepia images of an apparently crucified man. The image is similar to traditional *artistic conceptions* of Jesus' appearance. The shroud's provenance cannot be traced earlier than the mid-fourteenth century, at which time a respected bishop reported the artist who produced it had confessed. *Right:* A photographic negative produces a more lifelike image, although shroud enthusiasts err when they claim the image on the cloth is a "photographic negative."

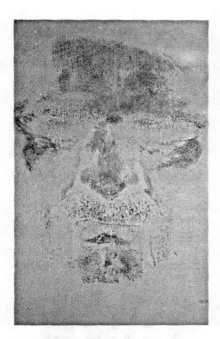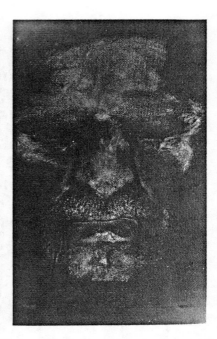

Plates 2-3. *Left:* An impression of the author's face, obtained by coating the face with a moist rouge and imprinting it on canvas stretched loosely over a frame. *Right:* A photographic negative returns a "positive" and more lifelike image. But note the serious wraparound distortions, an inevitable fact of geometry.

Plates 4-5. Positive (left) and negative (right) photographs of a *print* made by pressing cloth onto a sculpted bas-relief coated with a semimoist medium. The low relief minimizes distortions, but (unlike the shroud image) the tones are too uniform and the edges too sharp.

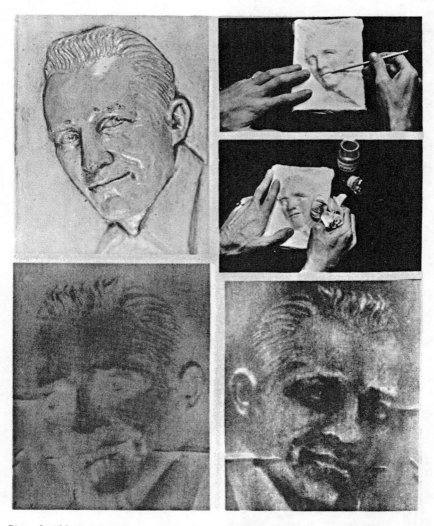

Plate 6. "Medieval technology" is demonstrably capable of producing shroudlike "negative" images with visually proper tonal gradations, softened edges, and minimal penetration into the fibers. *Upper left:* A suitable bas-relief is chosen. *Upper right:* Wet cloth is carefully molded to the relief; when it is dry, powdered pigment (in this instance a mixture of myrrh and aloes) is rubbed on with a cloth-over-cotton dauber. The resulting image (bottom left) becomes strikingly lifelike when it is viewed as a photographic negative (bottom right).

Plate 7. Negative photograph of the face of the shroud image.

Plate 8. Negative photograph of a rubbing image done by the author using iron oxide as the pigment. Iron oxide has been identified on the shroud image fibers.

Plate 9. Negative photograph of another rubbing image. In this instance the iron-oxide pigment was made by calcining green vitriol according to a twelfth-century recipe. The "blood" trickles were added with tempera paint.

# 9

# Medieval Negatives

Sometimes it almost seems that sindonologists have seriously considered the possibility of artistry, since they expend so much effort convincing readers that such a possibility is all but absurd. Thomas Humber warms to the task in the introduction to *The Sacred Shroud,* concluding it is "probably" impossible for an artist to have produced the image since he would have required "command of knowledge and abilities quite incredible for his time." Humber adds:

> Specifically, he must have known the precise methods of crucifixion of the period; he must have possessed the medical knowledge of a contemporary master surgeon; he must have utilized an art process unknown to any great master, never duplicated before or since; he must have been able to foresee and approximate principles of photographic negativity not otherwise discovered for centuries. He must have used a coloring agent that would be unaffected by intense heat. He must have been able to incorporate into his work recently discovered details that the human eye cannot see.[1]

"For many people," Humber says, "it may well be easier to accept the authenticity of the Shroud than to face the almost insoluble mysteries it would present were it a fake."

The first two of Humber's arguments (relating to the pathology of crucifixion) we have earlier shown to be ill-founded. As to "photographic negativity," we emphasized that, while the shroud image is a negative, it is not a photographic one. It is interesting to note here that

> ...the camera, oddly enough, was invented many centuries before photography. In the form of the camera obscura, it projected a view of an outdoor scene into a darkened room, directing light rays from the scene

95

through a small hole in one wall to form an image on the opposite wall. During the 11th Century a number of Arabian scientist-philosophers were amusing themselves with camera obscuras made out of tents. In the late 15th Century Leonardo da Vinci described the "dark chamber" in knowledgeable detail.[2]

Our photographic consultant, James R. Burke, called my attention to the camera obscura; and the artist-craftsman on our panel of experts, Glen Taylor—taking advantage of his home entranceway and door peep-hole, from which he removed the viewing lens—introduced me to its interesting effects. Projected on the opposite wall, although upside down, was a color image of the outside scene—almost as if projected from a color slide.

However, although the eleventh-century use of the camera obscura demonstrates that there was some projected light in the "Dark Ages," we must point out that it could not have been used to produce an image like that on the shroud. First of all such an image is not a negative. Even if one were to create a negative "transparency" (as by painting an image on translucent material and increasing the opacity of the highlights by painting them more thickly) and then to take advantage of the bleaching effect of sunlight on natural (brown) linen, the projected image is too dim to appreciably bleach the cloth (even in several years' time). One could, however, dispense with the camera obscura and, theoretically at least, simply place a full-size "transparency" in direct contact with unbleached linen and expose it to lengthy periods of sunlight. In fact, John Fischer, a forensic analyst on our team, used a simple cut-out paper shape to mask out an area of unbleached linen, which he then exposed to several hours of ultraviolet radiation. The result was a sharply defined image, the color of the original cloth, on a lightened background. While Fischer's experiment was in connection with another shroud-related issue (to be discussed in a later chapter), it did serve as a crude test of this possibility as well as to demonstrate further that the "random checkerboard" or "half-tone" effect (cited in the previous chapter) is not a characteristic of radiation-produced images.

We consider this hypothetical method of image formation to be far-fetched, incompatible with the image on the shroud (in several additional respects), and have included it here merely to stimulate the reader's thinking, as well as to consider briefly another hypothesis—that the shroud image might have resulted from the cloth's being exposed to sunlight beaming through a stained-glass window for a considerable period of time. In fairness to the professor of rabbinic literature who suggested it, we should note that it was briefly mentioned in casual conversation and, properly, as quickly withdrawn.[3] It is unlikely in the extreme that a stained-glass window would have a dorsal image head-to-head with a frontal one, and, in any case, any such sunlight-employed "photographic" technique begs the question: Why would a medieval artist even consider such an approach?

One of the earliest attempts to explain the shroud's negative image was cited by Canon Chevalier, the skeptical Catholic scholar who uncovered the d'Arcis memorandum and related documents claiming the shroud was only an artist's "representation." Apparently it was an M. Chopin who first advanced the hypothesis,[4] and it was endorsed by the noted shroud critic, Father Herbert Thurston, in 1903:

> It appears to me quite conceivable that the figure of our Lord may have been originally painted in two different yellows, a bright glazed yellow for the lights and a brownish yellow for the shadows. What chemist would be bold enough to affirm that under the action of time and intense heat (like the fire of 1532) the two yellows may not have behaved very differently, the bright yellow blackening, the brown yellow fading?[5]

In fact, something like this is actually known to have happened. In a fresco painting at Assisi, Vignon noted, and entire portion depicting a group of figures appeared to have been painted negatively. One portrait head was particularly striking in this regard, with the flesh tints having become "almost black and the beard completely white." When the fresco was photographed, the negative plate returned a realistic positive image as it must have originally appeared. The negative effect is only in a portion of the fresco and, states Vignon, "the figures below a sharply defined limit remain positive. The limit corresponds to a change in the plaster on which they are painted."[6] Obviously, the negative images were the result, as Vignon said, of "chemical change."

Vignon was correct in arguing that inversion of colors could not have been the cause of the shroud's negative property. As he observed, the shroud figures are monochromatic, formed, as he said, "in reddish-brown tints." Modern examinations of the shroud conclusively refute the color-inversion hypothesis, although it was something less than foolish at the turn of the century when access to a study of the shroud was effectively limited to the rather fuzzy Pia photos.

An argument is frequently proffered to the effect that an artist would not have produced a negative image, because to do so would be self-defeating; supposedly, medieval viewers would be unable to appreciate it.[7] This argument is easily dismissed: The historical record proves that pilgrims thronged to exhibitions of the shroud, where it was regarded with awe. Whether all grasped the idea (which a little reflection would have led them to) that simple contact would result in the higher prominances printing darker, or whether many did not, is entirely beside the point. The very strangeness of the negative imprint might well have seemed to confirm that the image was special in some mysterious way, prompting the credulous to believe it could only be the Holy Shroud of Christ.

In contrast to the opinion of many sindonologists, Vignon affirmed: "It is not absurd for a painter to reproduce a work in negative, but" he added, "if he had tried to do so he would inevitably have failed."[8] The reason a forger might have desired to produce a negative may be simply stated: to create—in the Edessan-image tradition—the effect of a body having been imprinted on the cloth. Simple experimentation (as we discussed in Chapter 7) would immediately show that such images have the darks and lights reversed. (The putative artist need not have thought in modern "photographic" terms at all.) We have seen, however (as an artist would have seen), that such images will be severely distorted—most notably in the image of the face. If, as we may well understand, this offended the forger's artistic sensibility, then he may have gone in search of a technique that would produce undistorted negative images.

What might this technique have been? Initially, one might suppose that a clever artist merely painted the shroud image, reversing the lights and darks. The assertions of sindonologists notwithstanding, medieval artists could and did create "negative" portraits. In *Art Through the Ages* Gardner reproduces an eleventh-century mosaic portrait of Christ from the Greek monastery church of Hosios Lucas (St. Luke), stating:

> At first glance one does not realize that the areas of the face which in normal light would be rendered as deep shadows appear here as bright highlights. This might be called reverse, or negative, modeling (as in photographic negatives). These mosaics were lit by reflected light or by torches or candles from below, heightening this negative modeling so that the figures seem to glow from within.[9]

Although the image reproduced by Gardner is a mosaic, it could easily have been a painting. Some of the early arguments against the painting hypothesis—that there would necessarily be brush marks or that the paint would flake off—today carry little weight. For example, the director of the Louvre's scientific laboratory, Madeline Hours, has commented on X-ray analyses of works by Leonardo da Vinci: "Photographs of details...do not enable the brushwork or the direction of the strokes to be traced."[10] And a dilute watercolor medium, such as tempera, has recently been used to produce paintings on linen that can—in defiance of Vignon's claims—be "folded, rolled, wrapped, knotted up and mistreated in any way, shape or fashion unchanged in appearance."[11]

However, there are other considerations arguing against the freehand-painting hypothesis, one of which is the fact that medieval tempera paintings were consistently preceded by a preliminary drawing (often fixed with ink).[12] Indeed, without some method of accurately proportioning the anatomy of two images of a man upon a fourteen-foot length of linen, it would be foolhardy to proceed. But no evidence has been discovered on the shroud fibrils to indicate any preliminary drawing was made, although there are possible ways around the problem (as for example, taking repeated measurements from a full-size drawing or statue).

Wuenschel cites a strong argument to the effect that the artist—lacking the benefit of a photo-reversed *positive* image and "doing everything in reverse"—could not have been assured of the success evident in the positive photographs of the shroud. He adds:

> And he would have to do everything with precision, for it is well known how little is needed to alter a beautiful countenance and make it a caricature, especially when its beauty is due to the expression.[13]

The point though is not that the artist would have foreseen the photographic reversal of his work, but that *we* see it and it is relatively undistorted—especially in the portrait of the face. Indeed, the mosaic artist mentioned rendered the eyes incorrectly (from the point of view of a comparison with the shroud) by rendering them in the *positive*. (His work differs from the shroud in other respects, and overall the work is exceedingly stylized and obviously "artistic"—unlike the more natural-looking shroud image.) Moreover, artists' attempts to copy the shroud image (with perhaps one or two exceptions[14]) have met with poor results when the copies were photographically reversed to positives.[15] To the best of my knowledge, no artist has succeeded in freehand-painting a negative image of a face that comes close to matching the quality of the shroud portrait—without "cheating" by working from a negative. (I say "cheating," for by copying a negative the difficult work is already done.)

In this context, we note the efforts of a distinguished shroud scientist, Dr. Walter McCrone, who, after microscopically detecting paint pigments on the shroud image, attempted to have a talented artist friend paint a negative:

> He did have some trouble because he's such a good artist he kept thinking in terms of light and shadow. Of course with the Shroud, you have to think in terms of what would a body under a cloth—how would that register on the shroud?...I couldn't get my artist friend to do this. Again he had trouble with light and shadow. . . . I'm sorry I got into this part of the controversy, and I wish that I had stuck to my microscope.[16]

While we should never underestimate what an unknown, skillful artist might be capable of—and so cannot conclusively rule out freehand painting—we must add that convincing evidence for any painting medium (that is, oil, egg tempera, etc.) on shroud image fibers is lacking. (Powdered pigment, however, is another matter.) Even at 40X magnification[17] there are no obvious encrustations and no apparent cementing between threads nor any consistent and confirmed coating of fibers to indicate the presence of a painting medium. (A contrary finding will be discussed in later chapters.) The superficiality of the stain—extending "only 2 or 3 fibers deep into the thread structure"[18]—is another strong argument against painting. A fluid medium (for example, paint, dye, ink) would be expected, by capillary action, to penetrate much farther—to the depth of a full thread, or even to the reverse of the cloth. Finally, tests at several laboratories[19] failed to detect the presence of any foreign organic substance in "body" image areas.

Vignon mentioned a quite different hypothesis—"so ingenious," he said, "that it arouses our admiration," although he did not credit the source. As he explained:

> Suppose we take a large blackboard and draw a figure on it in brown chalk. The chalk will stand out against the black background; therefore we can mass it thickly for the high lights, and let the black show through the chalk for the deepest shadows. The portrait finished, transfer it on to a white cloth by laying the cloth on the blackboard. Behold we have a negative.

Noting the difficulty of producing the modelled contours, he adds:

> We cannot *outline* the figure in chalk, because on our blackboard the chalk represented the high lights. This knowledge of technique is just possible in a frequenter of the studios of to-day; but such a complicated process as we have described would have been impossible for the painters of the Middle Ages.[20]

Be that as it may, it is becoming clearer that an ingenuous medieval artist had many ways of seeing and comprehending simple negative images. In fact, negative images are known from ancient times.

## Ancient Negatives

The earliest one of which I am aware, charming in its naiveté, was created by an early cave-dwelling artist who decorated the walls of his "studio" with two spotted horses. Surrounding the equine images were handprints— *negative* handprints, presumably made from life. The hand was placed on the cave wall and, stencil-like, color was extended over a small round area. The result was a blank, or negative, image of a hand.[21] Perhaps it is wrong to use the pejorative *naiveté,* since such an image reveals a mind capable of grasping a more complex idea than that of making a simpler, direct image. The artist of the Pech Merle Cave (Dordogne, France) had discovered for himself the principle of positive and negative, the cave-dark and sunlight of his magical imagistic world.

Whenever in his ancient civilizations man has sought to make impressions (as of a seal in clay), he has—not unwittingly—confronted the concept of positive versus negative. To make a stamp or mold, for example, one must decide whether the device will be positive (and the impression negative) or vice-versa. For instance, one may draw a simple shape, such as a circle, on a stone; he may then carve out the circle, creating a negative area capable of forming a raised, positive shape in clay. Alternately, he may remove the background from around the circle, thus "raising" it, so that the resulting form will create a negative impression in clay; or (how easy is the conversion) he can ink this raised form and impress a positive black circle on white paper or cloth. Yet again, without changing his imprinting device at all, he may obtain the opposite effect by using white pigment on black cloth.

All artists know the simple relationship between positive and negative and make use of it constantly—in sculpting reliefs, making molds and casts, even doing renderings in pencil or paint. This is especially true with printmaking.

The concept of printing may have derived from engraved seals[22] and is attributed to the Chinese:

> The earliest examples of true printing may be stones known from the Han period in China (202 B.C.–A.D. 221) on which forms were left in relief on a cutaway background. Such stones are known to have been used later to make patterns on cloth. The cloth was stretched over the stone and rubbed with a cake of hard colour as rubbings from brasses are made today.[23]

## Rubbings or Early Printmaking

It was in fact "rubbings from brasses" that came to mind when I first saw the shroud image. As I noted in my first article on the shroud,[24] I experienced something akin to *déjà vu:* I recalled the crayon-on-paper rubbings I had watched being taken from grave slabs when I visited Westminster Abbey. This technique automatically creates negative images, as one can demonstrate by placing a piece of paper over a coin and rubbing with a pencil.

But (in part because my background in printmaking techniques was rather limited) I first turned my attention to the later technique which developed from rubbings:

> True printing...awaited the invention of paper (also in China) about the 6th century A.D. In these prints ink was laid on the original surface of the block— the spaces between having been hollowed out—and transferred by pressure to paper placed over it by rubbing with some instrument, as the barren still used in Japan.[25]

Using a bas-relief of Dürer's "Praying Hands," which I coated with a moist rouge, I made a good negative image (see Plates 4 and 5). It had shroudlike characteristics, but the edges of the forms were too "hard," the tones too uniform, and the stain penetrated too deeply. Another problem was that I could not see the image as it formed and hence too much was left to chance. For these and other reasons—most importantly my decision to employ a *powdered* pigment—I returned to the oldest form of printmaking: monochromatic rubbing on cloth.

After some thought and preliminary experimentation I chose the "wet method," which is generally used for irregular, contoured forms although it is "considerably harder to master than the dry method."[26] I employed an available small, portrait bas-relief, to which I carefully molded wet cloth and allowed it to dry. Then, using a dauber, I rubbed on powdered pigment. (Originally I used a mixture of myrrh and aloes; I have since switched to a mineral pigment consistent with the findings of the recent microscopic tests on the shroud, to be discussed in later chapters.) The reader can perhaps anticipate how many shroudlike characteristics this technique (ignored by shroud proponents) might reproduce—some common to other techniques, some apparently not. (See Plate 6.)[27]

Such a rubbing technique automatically produces monochromatic negative images, and virtually guarantees that the photo-reversed positive will be of excellent quality. It possesses the requisite "inherent edge-blurring properties" and can give visually proper tonal gradations. Additionally, it yields images that are superficial (remain on the topmost fibers), highly resolved, and fire-stable. The images are—like those of the shroud—relatively undistorted, are "directionless" (that is, without brush marks), and characterized by "blank spaces" surrounding the forms. There is no cementing of the fibers, and everywhere the threads show clearly through the light-toned stain.

On herringbone-twill-weave fabric, other characteristics are noted, including a tendency (even with modern machine-woven cloth) toward changes in image density in relation to changes in the weave. According to a STURP report:

> An abrupt change in the [shroud] image density can be seen...at a single warp thread at the side of the face. The effect at this location has been mistakenly taken as evidence for a chin band. Such a change in density would not occur if the material had been brushed or sprayed, but it might be observed from a block print or rubbing where thread-lot thickness or surface discontinuities affected the amount of material transferred in the process.[28]

The fact that rubbings can share such a distinctive characteristic is highly suggestive. It is all the more so since under low-power magnification rubbing images show a "random checkerboard" effect.

Some additional macroscopic image characteristics may also be noted. For example, as with the shroud image, rubbings do not exhibit the texture typical of genuine hair or beards. And the sindonological question—"Why did the hair images follow the exact same law of intensity versus image as did the body image?"[29]—can be explained by the rubbing hypothesis, since "hair" and "body" are treated in exactly the same manner. And there are other similarities, one of which—an illusion of "top-lighting"—is especially interesting. As Vignon observed of the shroud image, looking at the photo-reversed (white-on-black) positive:

> The modelling is almost as if the light had been from the front. I say *almost* because some parts seem shaded as if the light came from above.

Later he says:

> ...the forehead seems in high light while the eyes are in shadow. This is because the eyebrows represent the point of contact, and the distance of the face from the cloth increases rapidly in proportion as the circular depression which surrounds the eyes is reached. For this reason the head seems lighted from above, although in reality it could receive no light at the moment of making its impression. It will be observed that with the mouth and chin also the light seems to come from above.[30]

A similar illusion of top-lighting is seen in the positive photographs of my rubbing images.

A "broken nose" is one of several shroud-image flaws that may be attributable to rubbing application. As a close look at the face will show (Plate 7), the fracturing occurs on a line (possibly a heavy thread) that runs across the entire face (where there is additional minor, image fracturing). Thus we have not an image of a broken nose, but a *broken image* of a nose.

The rubbing hypothesis may also help explain another sindonological conundrum. Says STURP's Joan Janney:

> I was looking at the shroud for an hour one night in Turin. The closer you get the less you see. How could you paint it in such a way that while you're painting it you can't see it? I'm not saying the shroud's authentic. I'm just asking.[31]

Mrs. Janney's question prompts at least two responses and together they seem to make a complete answer. First, the rubbing technique can produce images which are quite faint and can do so with a far greater guarantee of success than painting since the relief itself is doing much of the work (although the technique is not entirely "mechanical"). Second, her assumption that the shroud looks today as it did 600 or 2000 years ago is unwarranted. Vignon noted long ago: "Recent critics cite testimony to prove that the impressions in the Middle Ages were much more strongly marked then than they are now, but there is no means of coming to a conclusion on this point."[32] However, we can observe that early artists' copies of the shroud (there are none before the mid-1350s presumably because it had not been "discovered" — or created) consistently show a much bolder image.[33] If the image was produced by a rubbing technique such as I have described, then considerable amounts of dry pigment could be expected to slough off (no fixative having been applied, as is done today with charcoal and pastel drawings). Also the cloth is consistently depicted in the early copies as much whiter. In this regard we quote Ray Rogers of STURP:

> The rest of the cloth [apart from the image] is continuing to age naturally. In relation to the background the image is getting dimmer and dimmer all the time. Someday the aging fabric is going to catch up with it and obliterate it.[34]

As our photographer, Burke, points out, the visibility is a matter of contrast — contrast between image and background, not just how strong one is. But either can affect contrast singly: The image may *fade* (as by pigment sloughing off) or the cloth may *darken* (by some pigment powder being smeared onto the background as the cloth was repeatedly folded and unfolded, or by age that causes the linen to yellow). Certainly the latter has occurred and (insofar as we can judge from the artists' copies) so has the former. It is therefore reasonable to conclude that the contrast is much less strong now than in earlier centuries.

The most persistent argument against the rubbing hypothesis is that rubbing images do not fare well in 3-D reconstruction. STURP pitted a photograph of the shroud (known to contain tonal distortions[35]) against a photograph of one of my rubbings, a half-tone photograph clipped from a magazine. Burke insists that variations in delicate tones (upon which 3-D reconstruction is founded) can occur with different photographic and reproduction techniques, and he thus has grave doubts about this "3-D test." Dr. Mueller says of this particular rubbing:

> As expected, it exhibits the three-dimensional information it picked up from the bas-relief, but STURP's three-dimensional reconstruction from it is badly distorted in places. Whether or not this is a proper and significant test is highly debatable, but nevertheless STURP has made much of this "failure." It has used this one early result to dismiss Nickell's rubbing technique as a method a forger could have used. There is some question whether this "3-D

test" (actually a test for local consistency in tonal gradations) forms a proper crucial test of a method of image formation: The particular mapping function appropriate for the shroud image could be expected to depend on many accidental circumstances attendant at image formation.[36]

Even different-sized daubers can—as I've learned—produce markedly different tonal patterns. Among the many other factors that could influence 3-D reconstruction is that of contrast, the importance of which should be evident from the above. This alone might explain why a mapping function suited to a particular (aged) image (with "softened" contrast) might not be appropriate for a brighter and snappier new one.

STURP also argues against the rubbing hypothesis on the grounds that "[T]here seems to be no historical evidence to suggest that any such technique was used before the 19th century."[37] STURP should know better, both from my articles,[38] which its members reference, and from sufficient evidence supplied them by Dr. Mueller.

Let me develop the evidence. We have already seen that the Chinese used rubbings probably as early as the Han period (202 B.C.–A.D. 221). The earliest known rubbing dates from the seventh century.[39] Moreover: "The Chinese method of making rubbings was to place moistened paper on the inscription and then to force the paper into the incised lines by means of a stiff brush." When the paper dried, ink was applied by means of a silk tamper.[40] Interestingly,

> Some sources suggest that the practice of making rubbings was directly associated with ancestor worship. In the Orient the custom of visiting the graves of the deceased was difficult for those who lived at a distance; to enable such relatives to venerate the dead, they were sent rubbings of the gravestone made on paper, a practice which did not deface the marker.[41]

The technique became highly developed, "with masters making not only stone rubbings but also impressions from bronze plaques and other artifacts."[42] The dry technique, at least, "was used in Europe possibly as early as the twelfth century."[43] Perhaps a further quote will suffice:

> Although it never reached the prominence of wood engraving or painting, by the mid-fourteenth century the craft of rubbing had achieved a high level of technical and aesthetic perfection. Because rubbing was then, as it is today, primarily a means of reproduction, it never attained the status of a fine art. However, the practical role played by the technique was by no means minor.[44]

Is it possible that one role the rubbing technique played was in the creation of the shroud of Turin? Shroud critic Steven D. Schafersman says of my rubbing images: they are "identical, for all practical purposes, to those on the shroud." He adds that the technique "is embarrassingly simple."[45] It is indeed, although some may think that producing the original reliefs would be challenging. Glen Taylor made two reliefs of Jesus' face and each took less than a couple of hours. Since, as Vignon knew, producing a satisfactory image of a face is the most important and challenging test of an image-forming process, we went no further.

Taylor suggests that the easiest method of making a "twofold image" relief would not be a subtractive sculpting technique (such as chipping away at marble or wood) but an additive one: shaping the image of easily workable clay and possibly giving it a sealing coat of gesso. A couple of days to sculpt the relief? Two more to produce the image and add the "flagellation marks" and the picturelike "blood" stains? Or perhaps it would take longer. In any case such a postulated scenario makes a good deal of sense. The artist could work out any problems directly on the relief, making as many corrections as desired with trial prints on cheap cloth at each stage, until satisfactory results were obtained. He could then be quite confident of producing a good image on fancy—and more expensive— herringbone-twill linen, and he would need not fear having to make possibly tell-tale corrections on the image itself. Might not such a procedure explain what Bishop d'Arcis meant when he wrote that the confessed artist's "twofold image" had been depicted "by a clever sleight of hand" and was indeed "cunningly painted"—not merely painted, like any masterpiece?

Given a suitable relief one could of course make as many "shrouds" as desired, although it is perhaps going too far to suggest that proliferating copies of "not-made-with-hands" images (discussed in Chapter 4) were made this way, despite the attendant legends that they could duplicate themselves.

One further advantage of a rubbing technique seems worthy of mention, if only to disprove yet another sindonological claim of long standing. Wuenschel argued that an artist producing a negative image would never be able to see how well he had done, since he could not "foresee the invention of photography."[46] Or as Stevenson and Habermas are still saying (with their usual inaccuracy), he would lack "the ability to check his work or know his results."[47] If an artist, employing a rubbing technique, indeed wished to "know his results"—that is, see a positive (reversed) image—he need only have done as I did when I was asked to demonstrate the technique on the television documentary, "Shroud of Mystery."[48] All that is necessary is to substitute black cloth and white pigment and proceed in the usual manner. Thus one could have seen, centuries ago, a positive image, one that would not be seen again until Secondo Pia—his hands dripping and trembling— held his photographic plate to the light.

# 10

# Scientific Pilgrimages

## The Early Studies

Ian Wilson suggests that one of the earliest examinations of the shroud—not a scientific one, to be sure—may have been a "primitive 'trial by fire' "[1] He surmises this from some small, round burn holes, as from a hot poker, antedating the 1532 fire. (Their earlier origin is proven by their depiction on a 1516 Belgian copy.) Such a "trial," as a test of authenticity, makes some sense in light of the widespread early notion that Christ's swaddling clothes and shroud were reputed to be impervious to fire (noted in Chapter 5), as was the cloth he allegedly used to wash his disciples' feet.[2] But Wilson's notion suffered a setback when the 1978 investigation found what appeared to be traces of pitch at the edges of the holes, suggesting rather that they resulted from burning pitch falling on the cloth from a torch.[3] (We recall that at the early exhibitions at Lirey the cloth was flanked by torches.)

Nevertheless, a chronicler in the time of Philippe le Beau (1478-1506) mentioned that the shroud had indeed been subjected to a series of ritual tests. These supposedly consisted of boiling the cloth in oil and water and then scrubbing it.[4]

The shroud's first encounter with anything approaching science was in 1898, when Secondo Pia took the first photographs of the "twofold image." Writes Sox, "Unknowingly he had started the scientific exploration of the Shroud with the large 'reproducing box.' "[5] This was a useful step, since it served documentation purposes and provided important new information regarding the cloth's so-called "negative" properties. It also sparked scientific controversy, with Paul Vignon and others arguing for authenticity (based on rather vaporous claims), and Chevalier and Thurston, primarily, taking a more cautious and—ironically, since they were non-scientists—

107

scientific stance, all the while brandishing those damning documents. Due to their poor quality, the Pia photos served little other purpose, and several critics even refused to accept the evidence of image negativity, insisting the results were due to "optical illusion." One suggestion in this regard recalls the hypothetical "transparency" we discussed in the preceding chapter:

> The Shroud, having been photographed by electric light, transparently through its substance, the paint, even though white, being opaque, would come out dark in the photograph, and produce a negative effect.[6]

(Actually, the shroud was not back-lighted; nor would back-lighting have been possible due to the backing cloth.) On somewhat firmer ground, there was the assertion that the negative effect was due to overexposure of Pia's plates. Vignon conceded that such could happen, but was correct in insisting it had not happened in this instance. He cited other photos of the shroud—both by Pia and another—which included the entire altar and thereby proved the negative effect was confined to the shroud.[7]

Any lingering doubts were dispelled by the later Enrie photographs, taken in 1931 with Pia, by then seventy-six years old, looking on. Enrie's photographs—including a three-section composite of the full shroud, a close-up of the face, and an enlargement of the hand "wound"—utilized orthochromatic emulsions and (for some exposures) a yellow filter. While these produced tonal distortions (by emphasizing red spectral components in the image), the photographs also reproduced some of the more subtle details in bold contrast.[8] For the next few decades they served as the primary means for studying the image on the cloth. Even the weave was quite distinct and could be identified as herringbone twill. There were no obvious signs of painting per se—no apparent cementing of threads (except in the "blood" areas) and no brush marks.

Sindonology became more organized in 1939, when the First Congress on Shroud Studies was held in Turin. Some twenty papers were presented on topics ranging from pathology to iconography. One subject of debate was the question of whether the "body" had been washed. Prior to the congress, two Italian sindonologists, a professor Romanese and Professor Giovani Judica-Cordiglia, had obtained contact-imprint images from corpses whose faces had been smeared with myrrh and aloes, olive oil and turpentine, and even animal blood. Although their results were predictably crude, they were referred to as pioneers in the report published in 1941.[9]

The first International Congress of Studies of the Holy Shroud was held May 1-4, 1950, in the majestic Pontifical Chancellery Palace near the Vatican. Möedder came from Germany, Barbet from France, Wuenchel from the United States. Four Italians were present, including a chemistry professor who gave a general overview; a Vatican archivist who had searched for additional early documents; a sculptor, Lorenzo Ferri, who had carved a marble statue of the "man in the shroud": and, of course, the "pioneer" Judica-Cordiglia, who again attempted to explain the image. A Spanish sindonologist spoke briefly of his country's devotion to the shroud, mentioning a copy in Madrid that was supposedly pressed against the Turin cloth in 1620. A few papers were read *in absentia*, including one by a Czech doctor, whose communist government denied him a visa, and another by a Turkish doctor—apparently the sole skeptic—who argued the cloth was a forgery.[10] *Time* Magazine reported on the congress, asking, "How big was Jesus Christ?" And again, "Did he have a brain weighing approximately 1,492 grams?"[11]

The photographs served as the basis for many sindonological analyses over the years. For example, Ferri, the sculptor and professor at the University of Rome, argued from his calculations (taking into consideration the uplifted knees and "hunched" shoulders) that the man of the shroud was approximately six feet two inches tall. A Roman anatomist, Dr. Luigi Gedda, was in substantial agreement. He had actually taken measurements from the shroud in 1946 at the Abbey of Monte Vergine (where it had been lodged during the war) and concluded the "body" must have been that of a man at least six feet tall. Gedda also detected a "slump" in the figure's right shoulder and made the remarkable deduction that Jesus had been a right-handed carpenter![12]

Direct examination of the shroud was still not permitted, although Yves Delage had desired it much earlier, and this was again suggested at the time of the first congress. But, perhaps fearful of what might be discovered, Turin custodians refused all requests. It seemed that neither would the shroud come to the sindonologists, nor could the sindonologists go to the shroud.

## The Secret Commission

That situation changed in 1969. At 8:30 on the morning of June 16, a small group of people met in secrecy before the high altar in the Royal Chapel, where the shroud is lodged. After Cardinal Pellegrino celebrated the Mass of the Holy Shroud, a clergyman climbed a stepladder at the rear of the altar and took three keys from a little velvet bag. Long-kept secrets were about to be unlocked.

Pellegrino seemed an unlikely candidate to be allowing examination. He had, after all, shown virtually no interest in the shroud, even though he had been archbishop of Turin for some time. Yet when he was appointed by

Pope Paul VI, it is said the Pope insisted that in addition to his stated priorities "one more must be added. That must be the Shroud of Turin."[13] And now the keys were in hand.

First the grille was unlocked, then the inner cage, and finally the reliquary. The shroud was unrolled onto a long table while the ten men and one woman gathered round. Three of the clandestine group were priests, one of whom was a shroud custodian, another a press officer. Two had backgrounds in history, art, and textiles. Of the remaining half, all were scientists.

Humber states that it is doubtful whether we should ever know of the secret examination were it not for "a leak to a strange man who calls himself Kurt Berna or John Reban." "Berna" and "Reban" are anagrams of Naber— Hans Naber, a 300-pound pot of a man who would call the kettle black, deriding the Turin authorities for acting "like thieves in the night."

Although born to Catholicism, Naber became involved with the shroud only after experiencing a vision, a "film of the passion," in 1947. Jesus appeared (looking just as artists have always imagined him) and intoned, "I did not die on the cross." As he spoke, Naber jotted down the story of how—"lifeless, but not dead"—Jesus had rested and then "rose again." Sleepless for three days afterward, Naber quit his involvement with the black market and began giving witness to this "truth," which he claimed the shroud proves. In 1954 he published *The Fifth Gospel* with borrowed money, and sent copies to the Vatican. He was ignored and the book was a flop.

In 1956 Naber created "The German Convention for the Shroud of Jesus"—a "convention" with only one possible member besides Naber, a 75-year-old doctor whose first name Naber could not recall. By 1964 Naber had founded "The International Foundation for the Holy Shroud," refusing to reveal the membership but using the "foundation" to raise money. The following year "Reban" published another book, which was successful. An English edition was published in London; a United Press International dispatch carried his story farther around the world; and, in addition to his office in Stuttgart, he opened branches of his "foundation" in London and Zürich. Then in 1971 twenty investigators in a new Naber publishing effort charged him with defrauding them of $75,000. He was found guilty and sentenced to two years in jail.

But it was in 1969 that Naber played his most controversial—and important—role in shroud history. This time, at least, one of the anonymous people Naber claimed association with seems actually to have existed. This "Turin official" tipped Naber to the secret examination, and on the first of the three days of study he sent out various leaflets and releases claiming the church was going to alter the shroud somehow or possibly even destroy it. Ten days after the brief examination was completed, a surprised Vatican undersecretary was photographed as Naber thrust documentary "evidence" into his hands. This represented the usual Naber claims that Jesus was not dead when wrapped in his shroud. A UPI account of the incident reported that "Prof. Kurt Berna" had "submitted" the documents to the Vatican, which had "no comment." The Associated Press sent out a similar story but without "Prof." attached to Berna's name.[14] The upshot of all this, according to Wilcox, was that

> At last the Turin authorities were forced to admit what they previously denied. On January 6, 1970, Cardinal Pellegrino released through his Curia a short statement to the effect that, yes the shroud casket had been opened; and that no, the cloth had not been destroyed; and that experts had been asked to make suggestions how better the holy relic might be preserved for possible future studies.[15]

These "future studies" began in 1973 and—with the permission of the cloth's owner, the exiled King Umberto—plans were made to actually remove samples for examination. Again the activities were clandestine. States Wilson:

> So secretly were all the arrangements conducted that when, on the twenty-second and twenty-third of November of the same year [1973], the principal British and Americans interested in the Shroud were in Turin for the television exposition, none of them knew that the taking of the samples was planned for the next day.[16]

Not only were the results of this official commission withheld until 1976 (even, complained Umberto, from him), but the very names of the commission members were kept under wraps until that time.

The membership was substantially the same as that of the 1969 examination, although one member had resigned, another was dead, and several new experts had been added. The 1973 panel included (in addition to the three priests) the following: Dr. Giorgio Frache, a noted forensic serologist, with two colleagues; Professor Guido Filogamo, director of the Institute of Human Anatomy at the University of Turin, and his colleague, Alberto Zina; Professor Enzo De Lorenzi, head of a Turin radiological laboratory; Professor Silvio Curto, the distinguished curator of the Egyptian Museum in Turin; a physicist, Professor Cesare Codegone; and, again the sole woman, Professor Noemi Gabrielli, retired director of the art galleries of Piedmont.

Other members of the group, but who did not issue reports, were Professors Mario Milone, director of the University of Turin's Institute of Chemistry, and Giovanni Judica-Cordiglia, who had participated in the 1939 and 1950 congresses and was now director of the Institute of Forensic Medicine at the University of Modena. The latter's son, also named Giovanni Judica-Cordiglia, was included and placed in charge of taking new photographs. Consultants to the team were a Swiss criminologist, Max Frei, and the Belgian textile expert, Professor G. Raes. All but three commission members were Catholic: Frache is a Waldensian Protestant, Frei an Evangelical Protestant, and Curto an agnostic.

Some of the commission's findings have already been mentioned: the traces of cotton, plus the discovery that the image stain did not penetrate the cloth but instead was confined to the topmost fibers. We will discuss the tests of the "blood" stains in Chapter 12, and need only note here that they were consistently negative. In his report, Dr. Codegone recommended against carbon-14 dating on the basis of his erroneous belief that a large sample would be required. (When Professor Raes made inquiries to outside sources about having his small cloth samples carbon-14 dated, Turin ordered him to *return them immediately,* which he did.)

Professor Gabrielli—the commission's only art expert—stated her conviction that the image had not been painted but suggested instead that it was produced by a *printing* technique. Interestingly, she further argued it was not the same cloth that had been exhibited at Lirey, but rather dated from a later period. Curto, too, thought the shroud image might have been printed, and he leaned toward a technique using a model or molds. Microscopically examining some of the "blood"-area threads that had been removed, he detected two crimson-colored traces, which he believed were due to painting.

Overall, although few firm conclusions were drawn, the tone of the commission's report was moderately skeptical—considering the results of the tests of the "blood" and the suggestions of Curto and Gabrielli. This was not to be tolerated in silence; and so states Humber, "A critical study of the report was published by the International Center of Sindonology, which is tantamount to the authority that appointed the commission in the first place."[17] The rebuttal report faulted the commission members for not attempting to identify what substances comprised the (apparently non-blood) "blood" and the sepia stain of the image, as well as for failing to work in concert, and for not removing the backing cloth to see if the stains were as superficial as the excised threads indicated. Predictably, criticism seemed largely to be directed in proportion to the skepticism. Sindonologists were especially angry with Professor Gabrielli, of course, whom Wilson described as "eccentric" (because she did not agree with him?) and (because she is a woman?) "unpredictable."[18]

Max Frei's report has been cited more than any other—presumably because it was not skeptical at all. At first his report was withheld (it was not included in the 1976 commission report)—while an *erroneous* memorandum was circulated, quoting Frei: "I can state with certainty that the Turin Shroud dates from the time of Christ."[19] Apparently Frei was either "misquoted" or had withdrawn his statement, since Wilson insists, "Frei makes no such claims," and describes him as a "cautious individual."[20]

Retired from the Zürich police, Frei, who was chosen to be on the commission "because he had published an article on the faking of photographs in 1955,"[21] is now a freelance criminologist. His controversial findings concern the presence of pollens on tape liftings he had taken from the shroud in 1973. In addition to the expected pollens from areas from the shroud's known history (France and Italy), Frei supposedly found pollens from plants "very typical" of Palestine, as well as several characteristic of Istanbul and Urfa (Edessa). If true, however, the presence of such pollens would *not* prove authenticity, much less "date" the shroud to the time of Christ. They might, for example, only indicate (as suggested in Chapter 3) that an artist had purchased an *imported* cloth at one of the cloth markets in Troyes (near Lirey).

Sox mentions that Frei's work "has been criticized because he apparently uses no control samples."[22] Certainly Frei's report[23] mentions no controls (while giving much space to other dubious claims for authenticity). More important is that STURP also obtained tape samples (in 1978) and reported: "Very few pollen were observed on the tape samples in the present Project."[24] Moreover, according to an article in *Science 81*, STURP

> is careful to point out that from their standpoint, Frei's small sampling was not statistically significant. They say the pollens might have been carried by the wind or deposited by the shroud's visitors; its presence does not prove that the shroud was ever in the Holy Land.[25]

Shroud critic Steven Schafersman, a professional micropaleontologist, is even harsher in his criticism. Noting how neatly Frei's samples dovetail with Wilson's "theory" that the shroud and the Edessan Image were one and the same, together with Frei's endorsement of that view, Schafersman states:

> I find Max Frei's conclusions incredible. A professional palynologist [palynology is the study of spores and pollen] should examine Frei's original tape samples containing his pollen grains, examine all of STURP's sticky tape samples for pollen, and request that duplicate and independent sticky tape samples of pollen and dust be allowed by the Turin authorities. Most STURP scientists doubt Frei's work and discount his results.[26]

More recently Frei, who took additional samples in 1978, claimed to have again found numerous pollens which he asserted confirmed his earlier findings. In addition, according to wire-service reports:

He said he found traces of ointment made from a type of aloe that grows only on the island of Socotra, off the coast of South Yemen. Ancient texts refer to the ointment as having been applied to corpses before burial, Frei said.[27]

Frei reportedly presented these new "findings" to Archbishop Ballestrero (Pellegrino's successor).[28] It was just in time to make 1981 Easter news. But not even "traces" of this alleged burial ointment were found by the numerous other investigators. Indeed, not "traces" but much greater amounts should be present if such an ointment had been used on "the man of the shroud" — as Frei's alleged discovery is supposed to suggest. In short, none of Frei's reported "evidence" has credibility any longer. And Schafersman's call for an independent examination seems even more necessary.

*The STURP*

A new examination followed the commission's work — after a preliminary 1977 conference[29] and the creation of the Shroud of Turin Research Project (STURP), composed of some forty American scientists. The 1978 examination was timed to coincide with a new exposition of the cloth, the first full-fledged one since 1933. (The 1973 showing which coincided with the commission's second phase was only a television exposition.) In the six weeks beginning August 26 more than three million pilgrims filed by to view the cloth, which — against the darkness of the Renaissance cathedral and in its lighted frame — "appeared suspended in space, and illuminated as if from within."[30] The shroud had come a long way from its torch-flanked platform exhibitions at Lirey.

Among the pilgrims were the STURP scientists, including of course John Jackson and Eric Jumper, R. N. Rogers, and Samuel F. Pellicori. In their caravan were, as *Harper's* says, "sixty-eight boxes of fragile, glitch-prone equipment weighing six tons and marked with orange fluorescent paint." Late in the evening of October 8, STURP assumed custody of the cloth in the adjoining Royal Palace and began five days of almost round-the-clock testing. They were guided by a 63-page operations-plan booklet, which cautioned, "All team members should avoid giving the impression that 'the Americans have landed.' "

In the stately palatial hall once used by the Savoyards to receive visiting royalty, the protective red silk cover was removed and the shroud was attached with magnets to a custom-built rotating frame. The scientists and technicians began a preliminary examination. States Sox:

The first reactions from the examiners were fascinating. Jackson looked as if he had aged ten years having remained in the palace to oversee the first tests for more than twenty-four hours. At the Hotel Silea, where the American team was staying, Jumper was stating, "There's no doubt about it—it's a grave cloth!"[31]

Of the others, Wilson states: "As many subsequently commented, this viewing alone was sufficient to convince them that they were not dealing with a simple forgery." What had happened to due scientific caution? It seems the answer is that many of the STURP scientists had made up their minds before ever viewing the cloth. Months before Ray Rogers was saying, "I am forced to conclude that the image was formed by a burst of radiant energy—light if you will. I think there is no question about that." Roger Morris had added, "I personally believe it is the Shroud of Christ, and I believe this is supported by the scientific evidence so far." Robert Dinegar echoed this view, saying, "I believe it through the eyes of faith, and as a scientist I have seen evidence that it could be his [Christ's] shroud."[32] All these statements were made before STURP had conducted any tests on the cloth.

Such prior judgment seems to characterize STURP. Who are these scientists? Were they chosen by the American Association for the Advancement of Science, or some similar, independent body—picked *solely* for their expertise? Alas, no, although one could scarcely guess otherwise from press reports. Actually STURP's coordinators, Jackson and Jumper, are on the Executive Council of the Holy Shroud Guild, a Catholic organization that has been advocating what one Council member terms "the cause of the Holy Shroud"[33] for the past few decades. Jackson says, "I got interested in the shroud when I was thirteen or fourteen, when my mom showed me a picture of it. It made a great impression on me." STURP's Dr. Robert Bucklin is also on the Guild's Executive Council. Dinegar, who says of his work at a government laboratory, "I make bombs," is an Episcopal priest; he says his involvement with the shroud project "was the culmination of my career, being able to put science and religion together," adding, "whether the shroud is a hoax or not." He calls himself "an unbiased scientist." Rogers attends the church where Dinegar is assistant pastor. "When I first heard about the shroud project, I didn't want to get involved," Rogers said. "I don't like being identified with the lunatic fringe." (But learning of the 1532 fire changed his mind: Rogers thought the scorched areas on the shroud proved no paint was present, since he assumed that any organic binding medium would have shown tell-tale darkening in areas closest to the scorches.) According to *Harper's*: "With respect to the hereafter the group is an ecumenical one—among its members are Baptists, Lutherans, Mormans, Episcopalians, Jews, Roman Catholics, and agnostics."[34]

Agnostics? According to Schafersman:

Astounded by this revelation, I called a leading STURP member who assured me that, "yes, STURP did have one agnostic." One agnostic among forty scientists! What are the chances of randomly choosing forty scientists among the thousands in the United States and coming up with a group containing thirty-nine religious believers?[35]

There is no intention here to criticize individuals for their personal beliefs (after all, our team includes members who are Catholic, Protestant, Jew, and agnostic). But it is important to shed light on why a distinguished microanalyst was apparently "drummed out" of STURP after positively detecting traces of paint pigments on the shroud. As he explains, "they want very badly that the shroud should be authentic"—and this, he feels, has clouded their objectivity.[36]

Just before STURP began its examination, Jackson and Jumper had attended a Turin shroud congress, termed *La Sindone e La Scienza* (the Shroud and Science), at which a Spanish priest exlaimed of the "relic" that it "dripped truth from every fiber." He urged the participants to "just trust in what you see!"[37] He was, it seems, preaching to the converted: For example, STURP's legal advisor, Thomas D'Muhala expressed his initial reaction by quoting John 20:8, "he saw and he believed."[38]

What STURP could see of course was merely that there were no obvious encrustations of paint, and that came as little surprise. But obviously there were the rust-brown stains of the "body" image and certainly *something* had caused them. To learn what this something was, STURP obtained tape-lifted samples from several image, off-image, "blood," and scorch areas for microanalysis. Their locations were recorded as the tapes were stuck to microscope slides. These tapes were to yield the most significant evidence of any of the shroud's examinations to date.

Thousands of photographs were taken, including some eighty photomosaics in both black-and-white and color. Microphotos were made of the threads at low-power magnifications.[39] Ultraviolet and infrared photographs were also taken, and the entire shroud was X-rayed. To partially remedy one of the commission's oversights, a portion of the backing cloth was unstitched and STURP confirmed that the "blood" stains penetrated the cloth while the "body" images did not. Additional photos were made here as well, and a "micro-vacuum cleaner" was used to obtain debris from the back. Some other photography was done "on an opportunity basis" and included the taking of side-lit and glancing photographs.[40]

Several spectral analyses were performed, including X-ray fluorescence, UV-visible reflectance and flourescence, infrared reflectance spectroscopy, thermography, and spectrophotometry. Unfortunately the precision levels of most of these instrumental analyses were less than desirable—in spite of their formidable terminology. We will discuss the most significant findings (as well as some dubious claims) in the three chapters that follow.

At 2:00 A.M., Saturday, October 14, the STURP members completed their sampling and recording of data. The cloth was recovered with the red silk, rolled around its velvet-covered staff and fastened with a wax seal. Placed in its reliquary and protective outer encasements, it was returned to its niche above the altar. The scientific pilgrims set out for home, with their tape-lifted fibrils from the "relic," to assess their data.

All STURP examiners had been required to sign an agreement which included a "covenant not to disclose." Until October 1980 no articles were to be published or talks to be given without the express permission of STURP's Review Committee (chaired by Jumper).[41]

Yet consider these reported statements of STURP members made long before the prohibition to disclose expired (dates of publication are given):

• Stevenson (then STURP's official spokesman): "There is a strong sense that we're dealing with a potential impact that is incredible." He added that if the scientists had detected any evidence of fraud "they would have walked out the door long ago." (April 1979)[42]

• Stevenson: "All the evidence to date supports authenticity." (May 1979)[43]

• Dinegar: "I haven't seen anything yet that would lead one to think the shroud is not real. I think the burden of proof is being pushed on the skeptics." Stating that the image was not painted or stained, he added, "It seems as if it possibly came from some short-term pulse of energy. On the normal human time scale, you could say it was instantaneous." (May 1979)[44]

• Rogers: "These are scientists we're talking about. These are men who went to do a job—to prove that the Shroud was nothing more than a hoax—and they are coming away convinced that it is real, that it is authentic." (June 1979)[45]

• D'Muhala: "We all thought that we'd find it was a forgery and would be packing up our bags in a half hour." Instead, he said, "Every one of the scientists I have talked to believe the cloth is authentic. Some say maybe this is a love letter, a tool He left behind for the analytical mind." (November 1979)[46]

Note that we are not yet into 1980. Note also that it was apparently permissible to make statements to the press that there was no evidence of fraud, specifically no paint or stains attributable to an artist, but rather indications of some miraculous pulse of radiant energy having mysteriously formed the image. And note—in addition to the claims of prior skepticism—the *suggestion* that the scientists now believed the shroud "authentic," as well as the official spokesman's reported statement: "All the evidence to date supports authenticity." And yet at STURP's First Data Analysis Workshop on the Shroud of Turin held in Santa Barbara, March 24-25, 1979, according to H. David Sox (who was in attendance):

> For the first time, in the research on the Shroud, the discussion of a particular pigment had entered and apparently had been found. It was evident to all that this was going to be the important debating point in the months ahead.[47]

The microanalyst who had detected the pigment cautioned at the time, "Those of you who are emotionally wrapped up in the Shroud had better relax your emotions a bit." But it seemed the pilgrims would not hear.

# 11

# The Microanalyst and the Shroud

The scientist chosen to examine the tape samples obtained by STURP in 1978, the microanalyst whose findings would seem quite stunningly to confirm the mounting evidence that the shroud is a forgery, is Walter McCrone. His motto is "Think small."[1]

Walter McCrone has been termed "the best-known forensic microanalyst in the world,"[2] and again, "a well-respected and internationally known microscopist."[3] Even STURP's Ray Rogers, who has known him for thirty years but who now refuses to accept his findings, concedes McCrone is "the best in the world"[4] in his highly specialized field.

McCrone received his doctor of philosophy degree from Cornell University, where he studied under the distinguished microscopists, Emile Chamot and Clyde Mason. Subsequently he worked for a dozen years at the Illinois Institute of Technology. He founded his now-famous research company, Walter C. McCrone Associates, in Chicago in 1956. Under his direction, the McCrone Associates were pioneers in helping to solve problems with the ferromagnetic coating compounds that had previously caused extraneous noise on recording tapes. And much of the present-day work of McCrone's experts involves similar industrial matters—for example, detecting contaminants in manufactured products.

But McCrone Associates are also well known for their forensic expertise. For example, they were decisive in a criminal case, when they matched a tiny bullet fragment, taken from the left hand of the accused murderer, with an area missing from the fatal bullet. The evidence supported the defendant's claim of a struggle and he was set free. Through his complementary organization, the McCrone Research Institute, McCrone has taught numerous courses to crime-laboratory personnel throughout the United States, and among his "students" several have been from the FBI. Not only has he taught forensic microscopy but he has also written extensively in that field. In addition he has frequently testified as an expert witness in civil and criminal cases in both state and federal courts and for the prosecution, as well as the defense.

He has been employed by art galleries around the world to determine the authenticity of various paintings attributed to old masters; supposed "Rembrandts" and "Da Vincis" routinely pass through the McCrone labs. He once exposed as a fake a letter supposedly written by Christopher Columbus by demonstrating that the ink vehicle had not sufficiently penetrated and discolored the paper fibers.

His most celebrated work involved the infamous "Vinland Map." Purchased by Yale University in 1965, and purportedly drawn by a fifteenth-century monk, the map showed the American coast and indicated Leif Ericson had visited America some five centuries before Columbus. Arguing for authenticity was the observation that wormholes in the map exactly matched those of two known medieval documents, suggesting that it had once been bound between them. Too, the writing seemed genuine. Suspicious (and reminiscent of the shroud) was the map's lack of provenance, the dealer who acquired it refusing to reveal his source. Also a number of the map's geographic details were surprisingly "modern." As a consequence, McCrone was asked to determine whether or not the "Vinland Map" was indeed authentic. Delicately removing several minute particulate samples from the inked areas — samples together totaling less than a single microgram — McCrone employed Transmission Electron Microscopic Analysis. This disclosed traces of anatase pigment, which had not been synthesized until the twentieth century. The matter was settled and McCrone's reputation grew. According to Dr. Albert V. Crewe, who first filmed the movement of individual atoms, McCrone has at his command "the most completely equipped laboratory of its kind in this country or in the world."[5]

To some, McCrone's most lasting contribution to microscopy may be his multivolume work, *The Particle Atlas,*[6] a compilation of photomicrographs of various substances to aid identification. The atlas, which also explains recommended microtechniques, has been a continuing McCrone project since its first publication in 1967.

With such impressive credentials, McCrone was the obvious choice as an expert to examine the Turin cloth. His forensic qualifications and his expertise in identifying minute traces of pigments were important assets. From STURP's standpoint, perhaps, he was all the more desirable since he was interested in the cloth and even seemed to lean toward authenticity.

Following his participation at the 1977 conference at Albuquerque, McCrone accompanied Jackson and Jumper to Turin, where, says Wilson, he "was received cordially." Unfortunately, his desire to include carbon-14 dating as part of the proposed series of tests would result in McCrone's becoming a victim of Turin politics. He had been approached in confidence by the longtime sindonologist, Monsignor Giulio Ricci, who suggested that permission for carbon dating could be obtained by appealing directly to the shroud's theoretical owner, ex-King Umberto, in Geneva. Umberto did give his permission, but the fact that Ricci was a member of Italy's royalist party caused serious problems. As Wilson explains:

> It was not for his spiritual qualities, deep though these are, that [Archbishop] Ballestrero had obtained his million pounds' support from Turin's Communist mayor. With a pleasant air, and very much a man of the people, Ballestrero is not the sort to meddle with those wishing to return to the days of the monarchy.
>
> As events were to prove, during the exposition he was personally to reject permits of access to the Shroud granted in writing by the king. Effectively, by his mission to Geneva, McCrone had committed diplomatic suicide.[7]

Nevertheless, although he would not be present at the 1978 examination, McCrone was still on the STURP team.

Receiving the thirty-two tape samples, each about five square centimeters in area, McCrone set to work with his polarized-light microscope—the same one, he likes to point out, with which he began his career. The tapes bore surface particles and fibers from "blood," scorch, image, and off-image (control) areas. McCrone soon observed that several of the tapes also showed significant amounts of "a very fine red iron oxide" (ferric oxide, $FE_2O_3$), which he determined was "identical in appearance and properties (color, pleochroism, shape, size, crystallinity, refractive indices, and birefringence) to the particles of hydrous and anhydrous iron oxide particles, collectively known as iron earth pigment."[8]

To assess the significance of the ferric oxide, McCrone performed a "blind" control study, separating the tapes microscopically into two groups: those with the oxide "pigment" on the fibers and those without. (By "blind" study is meant that the microscopist did not know from what area of the shroud a given tape had been taken.) As a result he found that *none* of the control (off-image) tapes showed pigment particles, while eighteen tapes from "body" and "blood"-image areas showed significant amounts of pigment.

McCrone also noted that many fibers "appeared, in addition to the oxide particles, to be uniformly stained faint yellow to yellow." Therefore,

> To determine whether these fibers are also associated with the image we examined more than 8,000 fibers from both image and non-image (control) areas to determine the ratio of uniformly stained to colorless fibers. This study

showed that the image areas had many more stained fibers (30–72% of the fibers) than the non-image control or the faint image samples (10–26%). This shows that the image is made up of two components: an iron oxide pigment on the fibers and a uniform yellow coloring throughout many of the fibers.[9]

It was at this stage of his discoveries that McCrone appeared at the Santa Barbara STURP workshop with his preliminary findings. Some of those present asked him if blood might be transformed into ferric oxide under some circumstances. McCrone pointed out that the so-called "blood" of the shroud was chemically unlike that of an 800-year-old sample he had just analyzed.[10]

Because most of the ferric oxide particles were exceedingly small — generally measuring one micron or smaller (that is, being in the submicron range)—McCrone, Rogers et al. believed they were relatively modern in origin. This was because, STURP thought that at the time, "$Fe_2O_3$ in submicron size was not available prior to 200 years ago." Therefore, a *preliminary* STURP "overview" report concluded:

> If the $Fe_2O_3$ was intentionally applied it could only have been to enhance the image. Because of the perfect correlation of density with expected cloth-body distances and the perfect correlation with the yellow fibrils we cannot rule out some not-yet-understood natural method. We can state categorically, however, that no intentionally applied pigment was part of the original image (prior to possible enhancement).[11]

Still believing this was so (that the pigment had not been used to *originate* the image), McCrone stated in a draft abstract (November 1, 1979) that there was "no evidence for a [painting] medium in which the iron oxide pigment might have been dispersed." In other words, the pigment was merely that; it did not seem to have been mixed with a painting medium (such as oil or egg tempera), as would have been done to make paint. Sox explains McCrone's tentative opinion at this time:

> He figured that the particles were probably applied dry and dispersed by rubbing into the fibers. In a simulating experiment, McCrone prepared a finger-painted linen image area by rubbing his fingers into powdered jeweller's rouge and transferring that to a piece of paper which he rubbed out to a fair dilution. Then with what was left on his fingers, he applied the rouge to a linen surface. It was possible to build up images of any degree of density from near invisibility to deep red.[12]

(He employed the rouge because the ferric oxide particles he observed were "very similar to jeweller's rouge.")

McCrone himself cautioned at that time, with regard to the evidence for enhancement:

These conclusions should not in any sense be construed to cast doubt on authenticity of the Shroud. Our work leaves this question still as open as before we began. We can only say an earlier image, which may be real or artificial, has been skillfully enhanced with iron oxide particles. The temptation to enhance the very faint earlier image was apparently irresistible; the skill and restraint of the "artist" (and his choice of pigment and application procedure) must be admired.[13]

STURP, however, would decide not to accept McCrone's conclusion that the ferric oxide was a pigment, whether used merely for later enhancement or not. Rogers questioned the amount of $Fe_2O_3$ present, noting that the amount McCrone had estimated for both the ventral and dorsal images was only about 10 milligrams. Rogers found it "inconceivable" that anyone could enhance so faint an image with such a small amount of pigment. And STURP's John Heller attempted to find some other explanation for the ferric oxide. He began by observing that volcanoes and earthquakes and even micrometeorites and blacksmiths could produce iron oxide, including submicron-size iron oxide particles. Heller thus suggested that the iron might have been due to airborne contamination. Still later he would argue that the iron had been present in the water used in the linen retting process.[14]

But any such source for the iron would be expected to distribute the particles rather uniformly over the entire cloth. Other STURP examiners had conducted limited X-ray fluorescence measurements on the shroud and had found trace quantities of calcium, strontium, and iron. The first two of these appeared "as uniform background distributions," but as to iron traces, "their local concentrations vary." Most or all of the variation, they felt, was attributable to the iron in "blood" areas; and they suggested there was little if any difference between the amount of iron in "body" and background areas. Unfortunately, since the backing cloth had not been removed, the examiners noted, "Some ambiguity is therefore inherent in a full interpretation of the results."[15] And as a later STURP report conceded, "the precision levels of the measurements were rather limited."[16]

Samuel Pellicori said of the results of spectral reflectance studies: "$Fe_2O_3$ is not believed to be the colorant for the body image because it visually is too red, and its reflectance curve is different from that of the body image."[17] But McCrone was not saying the $Fe_2O_3$ was the *only* constituent of the image color; there were, after all, those yellow fibers; and it was becoming more obvious that they were responsible for much, perhaps most, of the visibility of the shroud image. (This seems evident from the photomicrographs.[18])

For his part, McCrone insisted that the red oxide pigment was found *only* on image ("body" and "blood") areas, and he emphasized that "there are iron oxides and then there are iron oxides." He stated he was certain the type he observed was not attributable to natural contamination since, as he said:

> It is very important to note that the iron oxide on the Shroud was applied as a very pure material. It is not mixed with other components of micro-meteorites, volcanic ash, soils or etc. It was at one time a powdered sample in a bottle or other container and consisted of orange to red particles averaging less than a micrometer in diameter. Its source was probably a natural pigment oxide. I had concluded early in my looking at the iron oxide on the Shroud that it was a synthetic iron oxide which was "invented" only after 1800. I now believe that much of the iron oxide I see is characteristic of natural pigment $Fe_2O_3$ that has been available for a long time. I no longer believe that this pigment was applied to the Shroud within the last 200 years; it may have occurred any time during the last 2,000 years.[19]

By September of 1980 McCrone began to suggest the cloth was a forgery. Speaking at a *closed* meeting of the British Society for the Turin Shroud (the *Catholic Tribune* broke the story), he said he thought the Turin custodians would have to decide to permit carbon-14 dating: "What I think is going to happen is that the Shroud will be dated," he said, "and that the date will be August the 14th, 1356, plus or minus 10 years. Mostly minus." Obviously McCrone could still manage some wit, although he stated he was tired of the controversy and would "like to go live on a South Sea island for a little while."[20]

At the meeting McCrone also began to hint that he thought he now knew what caused the yellowing of the image-area fibers. He was more specific about other discoveries: He had detected significant amounts of artists' vermilion and rose madder, he said, as well as trace amounts of still other pigments. These, he was soon to report[21] were ultramarine, azurite, orpiment, and wood charcoal—all known in the Middle Ages and suggestive of the shroud's presence at some time in an artist's studio.

Commenting on McCrone's talk to the British group and his reported identification of "red iron oxide similar to artists' iron-rich earth pigments," Ray Rogers was quoted as saying: "One theory was that keeping the shroud in an iron chest might have caused accumulations of iron oxide particles to gravitate to the image area, if," he added, "there was anything in the image area to attract iron."[22]

By this time, McCrone had already become persona non grata to STURP. In April he had submitted his two papers to the review committee, which promptly rejected them. The effect was of schoolboys lecturing the master. McCrone was told:

> Conclusions dealing with processes must wait for a summary paper which attempts to synthesize all observations into a single most probable conclusion.

This conclusion, then, must be compatible with *all* the pertinent observations. Contrary to your apparent belief, you are part of a team; microscopic observations *do not* exist in a vacuum. The very tone of your papers presents your work as the last and only word on possible hypotheses of how the image on the Shroud was formed.[23]

By "conclusions dealing with processes," STURP was referring to McCrone's argument that—since he had found not only pigments but, more recently, evidence of a painting medium (to be discussed in Chapters 12 and 13)—the shroud image had been painted. If presenting conclusions based on data was to be eschewed by STURP scientists, then one wonders how, for example, Pellicori's paper was able to slip past the reviewers. In it he stated:

Using the accelerated aging technique, natural perspiration plus skin oils, olive oil, and myrrh form visible stains that have spectral properties remarkably similar to those of the Shroud image. This suggests that contact with a human body plus the passage of time played a significant role in the later appearance of an image imprint of that body.[24]

Was Pellicori's use of the word *suggests* the only difference between his and McCrone's reports? Or was the essential difference that Pellicori was suggesting the shroud was *authentic* while McCrone was concluding it was a painted cloth?

In any case, with STURP refusing to approve his reports for publication, and with the "covenant not to disclose" expiring in October, McCrone then published his two papers in *The Microscope*. He was later to say he had been "drummed out" of STURP. He added that he began his work on the shroud wishing to authenticate it, but when the evidence pointed in a contrary direction, he had no trouble shifting his opinion.[25]

At the same time, STURP's full "Project Report," which had been expected to be completed by October 1980, would now be delayed for many months, presumably because of the need to assess McCrone's findings. STURP regained possession of the tape samples and began to make claims far different from McCrone's regarding the composition of the two types of images: the red "blood" stains and the yellow fibers of the "body" image areas.

# 12

# Is the "Blood" Blood?

Following Dr. McCrone's analyses—on the basis of which he concluded the "blood" is actually tempera paint—two STURP scientists tested the *same* tape samples and claimed that "the presence of whole blood was established."[1] To attempt to assess these astonishingly contrary findings, we must begin by placing the evidence pertaining to "blood" into perspective.

Proof that the "blood" on the shroud is composed entirely of paint, for example, would lead to the obvious inference that the image was the work of an artist. On the other hand, proof that the stains were genuine blood—even human blood—would not constitute proof of authenticity, since a clever forger might be expected to have used real blood. To complicate matters, there is the possibility, however remote, that genuine blood may have been touched up with paint in later years.

We have already seen that before scientific tests were done, based solely on visual observation, authenticity of the "blood" stains was alternately defended by proponents and challenged by skeptics. Whereas several pro-authenticity pathologists argued that the "blood" flows showed marked realism, Dr. Michael Baden, the distinguished New York pathologist, recently challenged their view. As discussed in Chapter 6, he found the "scalp wounds" especially suspicious, since the "blood" flows appear as rivulets on the outside of the hair, whereas, he observed, "When the scalp bleeds, it doesn't flow in rivulets; the blood mats on the hair."

We recall also the apt description of the "blood" stains as "picturelike" and the question of how dried blood (as on the arms) transferred to the cloth with such precision, or, alternately, how wet blood flows (which presumably

---

*Note: This chapter was co-authored by* JOHN F. FISCHER, *one of the forensic analysts on our team. See page 5 for full biographical information.*

would have dried and adhered to the fabric) could have remained undisturbed when the cloth was removed.

A major stumbling block to the claims of authenticity has always been the fact that the "blood" stains are unaccountably still red. "Carmine" seems the most frequent description of the color, with some preferring "carmine-mauve" or "carmine-rust."[2]

When STURP began its tests in 1978, according to Sox, two members "remarked on what many at the exposition had felt, that the blood marks were far more red than the Cordiglia colour photographs [taken for the commission] seemed to indicate."[3] The problem with the red color, as most readers undoubtedly realize, is that it is quite unlike old blood, which turns red-brown, then brown, and eventually almost black.[4] To such an extent are these color transitions characteristic of the aging of blood that forensic scientists have employed spectrophotometric data to assist them in estimating the age of bloodstains.[5]

Scientific tests of the shroud's "blood" stains began in 1973, when the commission experts removed several threads for testing. Microscopic examinations, conducted by Guido Filogamo and Alberto Zina, failed to detect corpuscles or any other identifiable blood components.[6]

A battery of tests on ten (4–28 mm) "blood"-stained threads (plus one control thread) was performed by Professor Giorgio Frache at Modena, whose laboratory is specially equipped for forensic examinations. Frache, a noted forensic serologist, employed several chemical tests, beginning with the preliminary benzidine test. Benzidine is responsive to peroxidase (an enzyme in blood) and the test is highly sensitive to minute traces of hemoglobin and hemoglobin derivatives.[7] The benzidine test and the subsequent, more specific tests performed by Frache were consistently negative.[8]

Frache's microscopic investigations revealed that making up the "blood" images, in part, were yellow-red to orange granules that failed to dissolve when treated with acetic acid or with oxygenated water or glycerine of potassium. These granules were also noted by Filogamo and examined at extremely high magnifications, but for the time being they would remain unidentified.[9]

Frache's further tests included microspectroscopic analysis and thin-layer chromatography. These techniques permit examination of extremely small quantities of blood.[10] Again, Frache's tests were negative.[11] And another commission member, Silvio Curto, detected traces of a red color which he concluded "must certainly have been added later and deliberately."[12]

Dr. Alberto Brandone of the University of Pavia employed neutron activation analysis, which is a nuclear (in contrast to a chemical or spectrographic) method of analyzing samples *quantitatively* for their constituent elements. According to one forensic text:

In fact, for the majority of known elements it is the most sensitive method of analysis known (a typical element can be detected down to levels as low as one-billionth of a gram). The method, when properly used, is so accurate that it is said to be 99.99% reliable.[13]

Dr. Brandone presented his post-commission-report findings at "The Shroud and Science" congress in Turin in 1978. He had detected a high content of gold in his sample, prompting the suggestion that the gold might have come from a previous reliquary.[14] This is possible, although so far as we have been able to learn the shroud's previous reliquaries were of silver, except for an iron box in which it was kept for a time after the 1532 fire.[15] Another explanation for the gold may be suggested: It was a common medieval artists' material—both as a powdered pigment and as gold leaf. It was used with red iron oxide, which was employed to tint the gilding adhesive and also as a polishing and coloring agent for gold.[16]

In any case, the most important finding of the neutron activation analysis was that, as Brandone reported, "what is related to blood chemically was not there."[17]

Subsequently, as we have seen, McCrone identified red iron oxide on the shroud fibers—dispersed rather sparsely in the "body" areas and much more abundantly in the "blood" areas. He found this oxide to be similar to artists' iron earth pigment "used since the days of the caveman."[18] As he stated at the meeting of the British Society for the Turin Shroud,

In none of the control areas did we find the *kind* of iron oxide that we found on all of the image areas. When I say the *kind* of iron oxide, iron oxide is a common contaminant in the world. There's plenty of rust. There are plenty of iron oxide particles floating around. On this table top, there are 10,000 of them—probably 30,000. Iron oxide is present eveywhere; you can't get away from it. But the nature of the iron oxide on the Shroud turned out to be very similar to an artists' pigment. Turned out to be—the closest thing I could find (we have a good collection of iron earths and iron oxide samples from all parts of the world)—the one that was closest to it was Venetian Red. I was a little sorry that it wasn't Turin Red, but Venice was as close as we could get. In any case, the particles were very characteristic of an artists' pigment.

McCrone added that all his work at that stage had been accomplished with a simple light microscope,

...an instrument that was no better, or used any differently, than Sorbet used over a hundred years ago. I'm rather happy about that because I've always been prejudiced against these big, monstrous machines, push-buttons, electronics, bells and whistles.[19]

But it would be the "monstrous machines" that would detect, in addition to the iron oxide, another artists' pigment: a significant quantity of vermilion (mercuric sulfide or mineral cinnabar). This additional work was conducted by McCrone, A. Teetsov, M. Anderson, R. Hinch, H. Humecki, B. Majewski, and D. Piper; the results were based on scanning electron microscopy with energy-dispersive X-ray analysis, electron microprobe analysis, and both X-ray and electron diffraction. Finally, a highly sensitive microchemical test confirmed the presence of mercury. As McCrone reported, "The artist evidently used a mixture of the two most popular red pigments of the 14th Century—a red iron earth and vermilion, a mercuric sulfide."

McCrone reached this conclusion concerning the vermilion on the basis of fourteen agglomerates found on a "blood"-area tape—unfortunately the only one still available to him (the others having been reclaimed by STURP) when he decided to conduct the additional analyses.[20] Thus, while there is positive evidence of vermilion in one "blood" tape, and plausible evidence of vermilion in all "blood" areas, it is not certain that vermilion was mixed with the iron oxide in "body"-image areas.

The same is true of a third artists' pigment he detected. He stated:

> I have recently observed more and more madder rose (a dye from the roots of a Eurasian herb), another red pigment, on the Shroud although this seems to have been applied not as a mixture with the other two pigments but separately. I find then that there are three different red pigments used, with iron oxide predominant but with significant amounts of vermilion and traces, at least, of madder rose.[21]

McCrone's evidence of the *separate* rose madder seems consistent with Curto's observation of traces of a red color, which he thought had been added separately. This observation is most interesting in light of the fact that red lake colors (for example, rose madder) were specifically used by medieval artists to overpaint vermilion in depicting "blood."[22] Moreover, red iron oxide and vermilion were together used for painting the "flesh" of figures.[23] And as one forensic authority notes, among the reddish substances that visually approximate blood are "vegetable colouring solutions like that of madder," as well as rust (iron oxide).[24]

Additionally, McCrone observed in the "blood" areas "numerous pigment particle aggregates that behave as though held together by an organic binder." Using standard microtechniques, he isolated fibers and particles, which he washed free of the tape adhesive and tested chemically. As a result he reported identifying the binding medium as collagen tempera.[25] Collagen (as gelatine) was employed as one of several tempera painting media in the Middle Ages; it was prepared by heating in water bits of old parchment and/or animal skins, ligaments, cartilage, and bone.[26] Such a tempera could itself have remnants of blood within it, but—given the high temperatures used in its preparation[27]—it is unlikely they would yield a positive response to tests for hemoglobin or hemoglobin derivatives. (In any event, the identification of collagen has been questioned—as we discuss in the Appendix; another possibility is egg tempera).

In marked contrast to McCrone's findings, Pellicori has claimed, on the basis of one doubtful analysis, that there was sufficient evidence "to decide that the material on the Shroud is blood."[28] As we show in the Appendix, such a conclusion is quite untenable from a forensic point of view.

The same may be said of the analyses conducted by STURP's John Heller and Alan Adler. To the best of our knowledge, none of these three scientists is a qualified forensic expert or has any prior experience in identifying bloodstains—in contrast, for example, to Walter McCrone and the commission expert, Giorgio Frache. We mention this because it is quite possible for scientists who are highly competent in their own fields (Pellicori is a physicist, Heller a biophysicist, and Adler a chemist) to make errors in judgment when entering fields for which they are not specifically trained.

For example, Heller and Adler first received a single tape sample which they tested, obtaining a positive reaction for some unidentified species of porphyrin (porphyrins are found in various plant and animal substances). Unfortunately the acid fumes used in their test severely etched the tape and so they were unable to proceed with the necessary follow-up test—without which it is impossible to determine if the porphyrin was a particular porphyrin found in blood. Yet the abstract to their report claimed they had "identified the presence of blood."[29] Actually, even a fragment of a leaf, for instance, could give a reaction similar to that which they reported; and so, we learned, can a trace of rose madder pigment in tempera paint. (Yet, curiously, when Heller and Adler obtained the additional tape samples from McCrone, they either decided not to conduct the requisite follow-up test or chose, for whatever reason, not to mention the results in their later report.[30]) Similar problems were found with their other tests.

They did find considerable amounts of ferric oxide and also a single particle of vermilion, the latter seemingly supportive of McCrone's findings, although not in the quantity he reported. Their lesser amount of vermilion may be attributable to McCrone's sophisticated instrumentation, which is much more capable of detecting the vermilion particles (among the similarly birefringent iron oxide ones) than was conventional microscopic examination, as McCrone himself found. We believe Heller and Adler gave insufficient weight to McCrone's findings (as in the instance of the rose madder). In contrast, we gave serious consideration to the possibility of artists' pigments being present in the "blood."

We researched medieval artistic techniques by referring to the available literature — including medieval artists' handbooks[31] — and by experimentation. This consisted of preparing various painting media (including natural collagen, egg tempera, acacia gum, and others) and of obtaining iron oxide pigment from hematite, ferruginous earth, and green vitriol (calcined according to a twelfth-century recipe[32]). Mineral cinnabar was also ground and levigated in the ancient manner to produce vermilion; and both madder root and genuine rose madder pigment were obtained. Oak galls were gathered and used to make iron gall ink (which seemed of interest in connection with the printing techniques mentioned in Chapter 9. Fish-bile yellow (known as "Lombard gold") and yellows from saffron and walnut bark were extracted, since yellows were often used in medieval times to "warm" vermilion.[33] These are only some examples. We also experimented with bleaching natural linen, and prepared linen test swatches to which we applied the various substances (alone and in different combinations), utilizing artificial aging techniques to observe their behavior.

In light of our experiments (see the Appendix) we observe that results similar to those obtained by Heller and Adler from the "blood" on the shroud could be obtained from tempera paint. We find many of their tests to be questionable, and we further note that not a single test conducted by them is specific for blood.

In summary, with regard to the "blood," one must consider all the evidence: the suspicious and "picturelike" flows, the red color, the negative results of tests by forensic experts, the positive identification of artists' pigments (most notably vermilion and rose madder, which cannot be rationalized as constituents of blood), and the failure of STURP scientists (their assertions notwithstanding) to prove the presence of blood. On the basis of this evidence these suspect "blood" stains have had their day in court: From a forensic standpoint the so-called "blood" is "non-reportable" as blood, and there is clear evidence that some — possibly all — of the "blood" is due to painting.

# 13

# The "Yellow Fibers" Mystery

At this stage in our discussion—with the evidence for artistry mounting steadily—it would seem that claims for the cloth's authenticity are hanging by the proverbial slender thread. Actually it is a plenitude of yellowed linen fibers upon which so much depends. That is because neither genuineness of the "blood" nor appropriate antiquity of the cloth could prove authenticity, since either are within the means of a determined and clever forger. For authenticity to be upheld, the *image* must be genuine; and the image seems to be composed primarily of yellowed fibers, sparsely coated with particles of ferric oxide. We have seen that McCrone found this oxide to be relatively pure and indistinguishable from an artists' pigment known as red ochre or Venetian Red, and that STURP has countered there is too little of the ferric oxide to contribute appreciably to the visible image. Dr. Mueller, of our critical-review team, states, "After reviewing the evidence on both sides, I *tentatively* conclude that ferric oxide contributes less than about 10 percent to the overall image intensity; but more experiments should be done." He adds:

My thinking is that, while the issue of visibility is important, it falls short of being crucial. What *is* crucial is whether McCrone is right in claiming that iron oxide particles are found only in the image and "bloodstain" areas and almost never in the clear areas. Because no conceivable natural process of iron oxide particle formation could so discriminate between image and clear areas, a reliable finding of iron oxide—*even in macroscopically invisible quantities*—only in the nonclear areas would be tantamount to proof that human artifice was involved in producing the image.[1]

STURP, it seems has not been able to disprove McCrone's findings in this regard, and Schwalbe and Rogers concede, equivocally, "the possible correlation" of $Fe_2O_3$ particles with image areas.[2] While we cannot do more than sympathize with STURP's apparent desire to sweep the oxide particles into some convenient dustbin, we must agree that the yellow fibers seem to represent the "dominant"[3] image element.

For his part, McCrone realized the importance of determining what had caused the image fibers to yellow. Although his "blind" control study indicated a correlation between the oxide and the yellow fibers, his first thought was that the $Fe_2O_3$ might have been applied to enhance a pre-existing image. We recall from Chapter 11 that—seeing no evidence for a painting medium—he felt the iron oxide had been rubbed on in powder form. (This was no snap judgment but the result of lengthy observation over a considerable period of time. Therefore, we will do well to keep in mind McCrone's *original* opinion—especially in the light of the controversy that we shall discuss presently.) Without an explanation of the yellow fibers, however, McCrone realized he could not answer the important question of authenticity. And so, he says, "I looked harder and longer." Finally, as noted in the previous chapter, McCrone began to observe larger aggregates of oxide particles that seemed to be held together as by a binding medium. Therefore, he says,

> I went back and looked very carefully at oxide-coated fibers for places I might see clumps of dry medium, places where dried medium coated a fiber or any indications of oxide dispersed in a colorless matrix. I know now this was hard to see partly because the matrix was very thin, i.e. a very dilute paint and partly because optically it tended to disappear in the mounting medium, the tape adhesive. But with a newly developed contrast enhancement procedure, I gradually convinced myself that there was something there.[4]

McCrone then conducted chemical tests on some of the fibers. As he reported:

> Histological stains used to identify paint media show negative results for drying oils and starch but positive results for tempera, a protein-base medium made from animal collagen, egg albumen or milk casein. Many pigment aggregates and many fibers from image areas were tested microscopically with amido black. Blue staining of thin fiber coatings, some blue patches of medium buildup and blue staining of pigment aggregates were observed, thus confirming the presence of a tempera paint. Colorless fibers from image areas and all control area fibers stain only slightly or not at all. Additional tests for sulfur-containing amino acids present in eggs and milk but not collagen were negative; hence the medium observed on the "Shroud" is an animal tempera, a common paint medium during all of the past several thousand years.[5]

Thus, according to McCrone, the shroud had been painted with tempera and the yellow fibers were simply the result of the tempera medium having yellowed with age.

STURP, however, did not accept this conclusion. They objected to his particular test for protein (see the Appendix), but much more importantly they observed that his tests had been conducted only on "blood" fibers — not on image fibers. When STURP's Heller and Adler conducted several different tests for protein, they too obtained positive results — but *only* in "blood" areas. (They also obtained positive results for albumin in "blood" areas and thought the proteinaceous material was blood serum; however, since egg tempera also contains albumin, one might simply conclude that egg, not collagen, tempera was the medium in the "blood."[6]) Other STURP tests (including mass spectrometry) failed to detect *any* foreign organic materials — proteinaceous or otherwise — on *image* fibers.[7] This is a very strong argument against the hypothesis — which McCrone had come to endorse — that the entire shroud image had merely been painted. Given the other arguments against painting (recall Chapter 9), including the fact that the yellow stain is largely confined to the tops of the threads, the painting hypothesis would seem to be insupportable.

But then what had caused the fibers to yellow? Ray Rogers, who had himself helped obtain the tape samples, had thought the tapes lifted more easily from image than non-image areas. This suggested to him at the time: "Something has weakened those fibrils."[8] In addition STURP noted that the fibers had a "frosty" appearance. As Schwalbe and Rogers state: "Phase microscopic examinations of fibrils from a pure-image area also showed well-defined surface erosion features [that is, pitting] which, we believe, give rise to the general 'frosty' appearance of the image fibers in the photomicrographs."[9] The observations of yellowed, weakened, and pitted fibrils were followed by chemical tests,[10] which tended to confirm the observations: In short, STURP concluded that the yellowing was probably due to cellulose degradation (that is, oxidation and dehydration of the cellulose).

Cellulose is, of course, the essential material making up plant cells, and thus textiles made from plant fibers (such as linen or cotton), as well as paper, are composed essentially of cellulose. Degradation of cellulose occurs naturally with age (hence the yellowing of the linen cloth in background areas of the shroud). Light, elevated temperature, or even the presence of foreign materials can also cause cellulose degradation.

What does all this mean in terms of the shroud image? It certainly does *not* mean the image is a scorch: We have previously detailed the objections to that hypothesis. The other class of possibilities for the degradation involves the presence of some foreign material — either transferred from a body in contact with the cloth, or applied by an artist.

As to contact, we have already discussed the failure of Pellicori and others to produce an acceptable image by simple contact. But while Pellicori cannot successfully explain the macroscopic image, he does score a point relevant to the apparent microscopic and chemical properties (that is, cellulose degradation). As he writes, with co-author Richard Chandos:

> The literature on cellulose chemistry and on textile processing indicates that cellulose undergoes degradation in the presence of heat or light. The addition of foreign substances that absorb the heat or light energy catalyzes or advances the rate of discoloration.

So far so good. But here is where the budding hypothesis goes astray:

> For these reasons, we have hypothesized that natural skin substances or applied burial ointments were transferred to the Shroud by contact with the body. These materials acted as the catalysts necessary to accelerate the degradation of the cellulose at those points where contact was made.[11]

Since the contact hypothesis is amenable to experimentation, and since numerous experiments by several investigators (including Pellicori himself) have failed to support the hypothesis, it seems that all Pellicori has established is this: Any one of a number of common substances—olive oil, sweat, aloes, lemon juice, no doubt even artists' media and/or pigments—can cause cellulose degradation. (Substances that are invisible when applied—for example, sweat—produce visible discoloration over time, or temperature, as the cellulose preferentially yellows. Pellicori slowly baked his samples of treated linen to simulate the effects of natural aging.)

A STURP overview report discussed this possibility of foreign substances helping to promote cellulose degradation, and agreed with Pellicori that the specific foreign material responsible "is not of prime importance," but need only satisfy certain criteria. Although the report asserts that "no traces of sensitizing materials were observed on the Shroud," it was suggested that "these may have been lost in time by chemical transformation, evaporation, or washing."[12] (We recall that early in its known history the shroud was reportedly subjected to a series of ritual washings followed by vigorous scrubbing.)

Since the contact hypothesis cannot explain the relatively undistorted image with its tonal gradations, we turn again to the possibility of artistry. Could an artist have added some "foreign substance" that acted as a "sensitizing material" and degraded the cellulose? Schwalbe and Rogers concede:

> If the image were the result of cellulose degradation processes, the possibility cannot be discounted that the Shroud was artificially imprinted with a cloth-sensitizing material and the image subsequently developed, perhaps by baking as Pellicori has described.[13]

As one "possibility" in this regard they cite the author's rubbing technique (discussed in Chapter 10) and state:

> Although microscopic examination of the Shroud shows that the image does not consist of powdered pigments, any of a number of cellulose-sensitizing materials could have been used instead. One may postulate that the image was developed as the deformed cloth material was ironed flat, baked, or exposed to the sun for some period of time.[14]

We need not postulate such an invisible-ink process (the difficulty can be imagined: "Did I put enough on the nose? Did I remember to do the left arm?"); and an " 'acid-painting' hypothesis"[15] is even more bizarre (as those who discuss it seem to agree). But we *can* reasonably suggest that some colored medium was applied (as by rubbing) and that the medium produced the cellulose degradation over time.

In fact Dr. Mueller has advocated formulating "a human-artifice hypothesis consistent with the known principles of art and science and also consistent with the observations of STURP, McCrone, and Nickell." As he suggested:

> First, the image-forming method will probably have to be based on some kind of imprinting technique to impart photonegativity automatically—most likely rubbing, à la Nickell. Second, the rubbing medium must be dry or semi-solid (to limit image depth), must contain a coloring pigment (probably an iron earth), and must largely disappear (being nonproteinaceous would help, relative to STURP's tests) by reacting with cellulose over time and temperature, or perhaps by evaporation, leaving finally only dehydrated cellulose fibrils coated sparsely with iron oxide particles.[16]

Dr. Mueller urged STURP to subject this hypothesis to "serious and careful testing" and to make "a bona fide commitment to trying to show how an artist might have forged" the shroud image. Our critical-review team (of which Dr. Mueller is a founding member) has long been working on image-related problems. Three of us have now formed an ad hoc subcommittee to begin to address the specific issue of the yellow fibers. In addition to Dr. Mueller, there is John Fischer, who did most of the lab work, and the author.

In the previous chapter we mentioned some of the experiments we had already conducted with medieval artists' materials. With regard to "the yellow fibers mystery," we began to rethink the problem and attempted to free ourselves from as many preconceptions as possible. And we began to investigate the causes of cellulose degradation and the effects of pigments on cellulose.

Fischer called attention to possible photochemical reactions[17] as well as to the various chemical substances already identified on the shroud—notably calcium and iron oxide, possibly a soluble iron salt[18] as well, plus trace amounts (at least in one "blood"-area sample) of mercury, sodium, magnesium, aluminum, phosphorus, potassium, sulfur, chlorine, copper, silicon, and titanium.[19] But he cautioned against thinking in terms of an "alphabet soup," with any desired chemical compound being inherently available. The one compound known to be present in significant amounts (and in association with the yellow image fibers) was, of course, the ferric oxide.

In our research we did not have to look far to find that *traces of iron in or on cellulosic material*

...are capable of catalyzing sulfur dioxide gas into sulphuric acid. Reaction between this gas and the oxygen and water vapors present in the atmosphere also forms sulphuric acid, which is extremely harmful to paper [that is, cellulose], acting as a catalyst, removing the water molecule from within the cellulose molecule or causing mild oxidation which results in the cleavage or degradation of the molecule.[20]

Along relevant lines, one authority[21] notes the "harmful" effects of rust stains (ferric oxide) on fabric, without elaborating, but another[22] mentions that (in the bleaching of cotton) "small holes may be due to the local catalytic effect of small rust particles, in promoting local oxidation." (One is reminded of the pitted, "frosty" fibrils observed by STURP: Might not the pitting have resulted from the ferric oxide particles having promoted local oxidation? If so, perhaps many of the $Fe_2O_3$ particles have subsequently sloughed off.)

An authoritative text cites the ability of "impurities like iron" to "discolor" flax (from which linen is made), adding: "The water of the River Lys in Belgium is especially adaptable...";[23] and elsewhere we learn that a "yellow-tint is characteristic of flax retted in the river Lys."[24]

Certain inks—such as medieval iron-gall ink—are acidic, and consequently can have a marked degradative effect on cellulose.[25] As yet another instance of the effects of iron on linen, we might mention the brown spotting which everyone has seen on the paper in old books. Known as "foxing," this is due to chemical action between iron impurities and organic acids released by fungi. It is worth adding that "[T]hese spots are independent of the mould growth and may occur even though the conditions which favor growth of fungi have been eliminated."[26]

The foregoing examples are not intended to represent hypotheses we are advocating (we do not suggest the shroud image is the result of foxing, for instance), but are intended only as introductory considerations and as illustrative of the importance of iron in promoting reactions involving cellulosic material.

To now attempt a more specific hypothesis, we might begin by recalling that the oxide pigment described by McCrone was relatively pure (whereas there are earthy forms of the pigment containing varying amounts of clay and silica[27]) and that in his opinion it resembled either jeweller's rouge or Venetian Red. Of the latter, one authoritative text states: "Formerly a natural oxide, partially hydrated, today it is obtained by calcining a mixture of copperas (ferrous sulfate) and whiting (calcium carbonate)."[28] Although today's Venetian Red contains only 50% or less ferric oxide (the remainder being a mixture of calcium carbonate and calcium sulfate), the natural form could be relatively pure.

Interestingly, we found a twelfth-century recipe for making red iron oxide (rouge) from green vitriol. (Green vitriol is identical to the "copperas" mentioned above. Chemically it is ferrous sulfate, or the mineral melanterite.) As described by the monk Theophilus,[29] the green vitriol was placed in an earthenware dish and calcined (that is, oxidized) by placing the dish beneath hot coals and blowing "with the bellows until it is burnt and turns a reddish color."[30] The ferrous sulfate oxidizes to ferric oxide; but we found that, even after washing, significant amounts of residual ferrous sulfate can remain.

Such ferrous salts, it is well known, are "characterized by their reducing power."[31] Our experiments showed that in the presence of moisture this ferric oxide (but ferrous-salt-containing) pigment is acidic and has a definite degradative effect on linen, producing weakened, degraded, yellow fibers. We mention moisture, since its effects have often been ignored in attempts—such as those of Pellicori—to simulate the effects of age by slow baking. Mere baking does not adequately involve the presence of oxygen and water vapor, which "profoundly influences many photochemical reactions."[32]

The medieval iron pigment which we have described is primarily composed, of course, of various hydrated forms of $Fe_2O_3$. Depending on grinding and levigation (fractional sedimentation, employed in the Middle Ages to obtain fine particle size[33]), this can have a significant number of particles measuring in the submicron range. Used directly as a powder, this pigment is most suitable for producing artistic rubbing images, and experimentation has shown a tendency for the larger particles to slough off more readily. Since submicron-size particles are known to cling nonpreferentially to virtually anything, it could be expected that over time the amount of ferric oxide would diminish and the particle size tend more uniformly toward the submicron range. Also, the possibility that the shroud was washed cannot be overlooked. David Sox asks in this regard, "Are we looking at an image, not burned by heat into a cloth, but almost washed out of it?"[34]

With regard to the minimal depth of penetration of the yellow "stain," two things may be said. The first is that an applied powdered pigment with a *minimal* amount of residual ferrous sulfate could be expected to cause only the minimal penetration observed. The other factor to be considered is the possibility, mentioned by another investigator, that the relatively large amounts of calcium could "have buffered certain types of reactions and, thereby, assisted in confining the discoloration to the tops of the thread crowns."[35]

Without necessarily excluding other types of ferric oxide pigments (for example, iron earth) we feel that the most plausible explanation for the yellow fibers on the shroud image is that they are the result of cellulose degradation and could have resulted from an applied pigment such as we have described.

One may wonder why we were able to find a plausible explanation for the cellulose degradation while STURP could not. Apparently, because they were unable to conceive of a viable image-forming process that would be consistent with authenticity, STURP scientists were unwilling to seriously consider a process that had been offered to them and a "sensitizing material" that was, in effect, staring them in the face. To have done so would have been to concede what they apparently cannot: that only hypotheses based on artistic work can explain the image on the shroud.

# 14

# Summation and Aftermath

As the (red ochre) dust settles briefly over Sindondom, it becomes clear there are only two choices: Either the shroud is authentic (naturally or supernaturally produced by the body of Jesus) or it is a product of human artifice. Asks Steven Schafersman:[1]

> Is there a possible third hypothesis? No, and here's why. Both Wilson[2] and Stevenson and Habermas[3] go to great lengths to demonstrate that the man imaged on the shroud must be Jesus Christ and not someone else. After all, the man on *this* shroud was flogged, crucified, wore a crown of thorns, did not have his legs broken, was nailed to the cross, had his side pierced, and so on. Stevenson and Habermas[4] even calculate the odds as 1 in 83 million that the man on the shroud is not Jesus Christ (and they consider this a very conservative estimate). I agree with them on all of this. If the shroud is authentic, the image is that of Jesus.

So what is the truth? Is the shroud of Turin genuine or spurious? Relic or rendering? Let us briefly review the evidence.

## Provenance

Nowhere in the New Testament is there mention of Christ's shroud having been imprinted with his "portrait," or any indication that his burial clothes were even preserved. There is, in fact, no record of the shroud of Turin before its appearance in the mid-1350s — at which time a respected bishop claimed it had been "cunningly painted" and that the artist had been discovered and had confessed. Although the shroud's first owner had ample opportunity to explain how he had aquired the most important "relic"

141

in Christendom, he maintained silence. Pope Clement VII judged the evidence and concluded the shroud was an artist's "representation."

## Jewish Burial

The use of a single large cloth to wrap a body for burial is atypical, to say the least, of early Jewish practice. The Gospel of John gives the most detailed account of Christ's burial, clearly referring to *multiple* cloths, with a separate "napkin" over the face. The body, he says, was wound "in linen clothes with the spices" (myrrh and aloes), which is consistent with his statement that Jesus was buried "as the manner of the Jews is to bury." If this statement is true, it also means that Jesus' body would have first been washed, in contrast to the "body" of the man of the shroud (witness the dried "blood" on the arms). The shroud is simply not consistent with John's account of Jesus' burial; yet if sindonologists refuse to believe John concerning these details, it seems they can scarcely rely on him for others. For example, *only* John mentions the piercing of the side.

## Iconography

As St. Augustine lamented in the early fifth century, it is impossible to know what Christ actually looked like. Indeed, the earliest portraits (dating from the third century) depict a beardless, Apollo-like youth; but this concept would soon be paralleled by a more Semitic representation (with long flowing hair and beard and a prominent nose), and it was the latter tradition that became conventional in art. It is therefore most suspicious that a "shroud"—its whereabouts unrecorded for 1300 years—should suddenly appear, bearing an image of Christ looking exactly like artists had come to imagine him. Moreover, the shroud seems the culmination of a lengthy tradition of "not-made-with-hands" portraits of Christ. From the sixth century came images reputedly imprinted by the "bloody sweat" of the *living* Christ, and by the twelfth century there were accounts of Christ having pressed "the length of his whole body" upon a cloth. Already (by the eleventh century) artists had begun to represent a double-length (but non-imaged) shroud in paintings of the Lamentation and Deposition; and by the thirteenth century we find ceremonial shrouds bearing full-length images of Christ's body in death. In these the hands are folded over the loins (an artistic motif dating from the eleventh century).

From an iconographic point of view, these various traditions come together in the shroud of Turin and suggest that it is the work of an artist of the thirteenth century or later. The shroud's provenance suggests a mid-fourteenth-century date, and the weave and condition of the cloth are more in keeping with a fourteenth, rather than a first, century origin.

## "Medical" Evidence

Several proauthenticity pathologists have been impressed with what they regard as the "anatomical realism" and the accurate "blood" flows depicted on the shroud. In fact there are anatomical flaws (for example, one arm is longer than the other), but the *relative* lack of distortion argues against authenticity and in favor of artistry. The distinguished New York pathologist, Dr. Michael M. Baden, doubts that the shroud ever contained a corpse. "Human beings don't produce this kind of pattern," he states. He finds the "blood" flows especially suspicious, particularly the rivulets on the outside of the locks of hair. In reality, he notes, blood would mat the hair. The hair itself appears unnatural, seeming—as Vignon admitted—"stiffened and thickened." Other details are suggestive. If we accept (with most sindonologists) that the position of the feet implies they were nailed together rather than separately, we must note that that is a European artistic concept that had become conventional by the fourteenth century. Also the shroud depicts the lance wound in Christ's right side, where artists invariably placed it, although only the Gospel of John mentions this wound, and does not specify which side was pierced. The thin, elongated features of the man of the shroud have led one proauthenticity pathologist to suggest Christ had a rare disease, yet such a depiction is merely characteristic of medieval Gothic art.

## Image Formation

There are only three classes of possibilities for the formation of the image on the shroud: (1) unaided natural processes transferring the image from body to cloth; (2) supernatural means; or (3) human artifice. We need not repeat all the arguments here; it will suffice to point out that authenticity advocates—their heroic efforts notwithstanding—have been unable to account for the image on the shroud by *any* process falling into the first category. Positing supernatural means is completely unwarranted and unscientific. While the shroud image's quasi-negative property has been argued as proof against artistry, in fact quasi-negatives have been known to artists from ancient times. Without excluding other potential methods of artifice, we note that a rubbing technique is capable of producing numerous shroudlike characteristics, including photonegativity. It seems that no other technique has yet been demonstrated which will so closely replicate the image on the shroud.

## The "Blood"

The nature of the "blood" stains has obvious implications to the question of authenticity, although a clever forger could certainly have used real blood.

While STURP claims that "the presence of whole blood" has been "established" by their tests, this claim is unwarranted. Many of their tests are questionable, and *none is specific for blood.* Results similar to theirs could be obtained from tempera paint. To these arguments must be added the other evidence against the geniuneness of the "blood": the suspiciously still red and "picturelike" flows, the negative results of numerous tests by qualified forensic experts, and the positive identification of artists' pigments, including red ochre, vermilion, and rose madder. Forensically speaking, the so-called "blood" is "non-reportable" as such, and there is clear evidence that some—possibly all—of the "blood" is the result of painting.

### Microscopic Image Properties

Viewed microscopically, the shroud image is seen to be composed of yellowed fibers, sparsely coated with iron oxide particles. This oxide, according to a distinguished microanalyst, has properties identical with an artists' pigment generally known as red ochre or Venetian Red. He concluded the yellow staining was due to a tempera medium that had yellowed with age, but other tests show that a more likely explanation is cellulose degradation. Since at least one variety of medieval red-ochre pigment can promote cellulose degradation, the presence of such an applied pigment would seem the most plausible explanation for the oxide-coated yellow fibers. Whereas fluid media (paints, dyes, inks) would be expected to penetrate well into the threads, perhaps even through the cloth, the pigment could have been rubbed on in powder form, thus producing only minimal stain penetration, just as is found on the shroud.

In summary, the historical, gospel, iconographic, pathological, physical, and chemical evidence against the cloth of Lirey seems overwhelming. And yet—while (to its credit) STURP has never asserted the cloth is the actual burial shroud of Jesus—some STURP scientists, many other sindonologists, and the authors of several hopelessly biased articles and books have implied as much. As Schafersman explains this implicit argument: "since [the shroud] isn't an artist's forgery, it must somehow be authentic, although we can't explain how, and if it's authentic, it must be the actual shroud of Jesus Christ, although we can never be sure."[5] The effect of such an argument—presented with more subtlety of course—is to potentially mislead those who are unaware of the evidence for artistry.

In fact, evidence for artistry has even been cleverly turned around and presented so as to further mislead the uninformed. Witness the recent alleged "discoveries" of Professor Allan Whanger, a geriatric psychiatrist at Duke University (certainly *not* an iconographer). Whanger compared the likeness of the shroud portrait to a *sixth*-century Byzantine icon and a *seventh-*

century Byzantine coin and argued (with Ian Wilson) that the icon and coin were copied from the shroud.[6] But since there is not a shred of evidence that the Turin cloth existed prior to the fourteenth century, the more sensible and probable conclusion is that the putative shroud artist simply copied the conventional likeness.

Far sillier are the claims made in an advertisement[7] for a "miracle cloth" printed with the shroud image. At first look, the ad seems merely a piece of satire; but if the sellers are laughing it is while en route to the bank. The ad informs that the replica is "Guaranteed the Most Powerful Miracle Cloth Ever Created," adding:

> The "Shroud" is the only cloth that has ever been accredited with possessing astonishing powers so strong, it was once draped over a dead man who immediately revived as reported by Dr. Paul Vignon in his book "The Shroud of Christ."

The ad continues with the wonderful news that "you do not have to just read about other peoples [sic] miracles. You can have them for your own self." It goes on in this semiliterate fashion:

> ...this miracle image is on such fine linen cloth that it can very easily be folded down as small as a pocket check book, so that you can take it with you to win at bingo, the races, card games, the casino and other games of chance. Take it with you to buy your lottery tickets and touch it to your entry form when you enter a sweepstake or contest. You will win or your money back.... Money will come to you as it never has before.

In all fairness, we note that many authenticity advocates agree with Stevenson and Habermas, who decry such "out and out abuse of the Shroud." They lament that "when the ad first appeared, an evangelical group that had offered to help raise funds for the Shroud of Turin Research Project quickly backed out."[8]

But now Stevenson and Habermas are themselves accused of abuse—of one kind or another. States Dr. Mueller, "Their book is replete with one or more serious misrepresentations—both subtle and gross—on almost every page."[9] And a *Los Angeles Times* review observed, "The evidence is not as fully convincing as they make it appear."[10] Schafersman terms the book "a classic twentieth-century example of pseudoscience."[11]

STURP is especially unhappy with the book (which employs "science" to argue that the shroud was produced miraculously) and has asked Stevenson to resign as spokesman for the group. (Apparently he has refused.) Habermas, a teacher of apologetics at Jerry Falwell's Liberty Baptist College in Lynchburg, Virginia, has not been asked to resign since STURP disputes that he was ever a member. (The book's dust-jacket describes him as a "research consultant" to the Project, but apparently he consulted only with Stevenson.) STURP also initiated legal proceedings[12] to force the book's publisher to include the following notice with each copy sold:

---

### CLARIFICATION

*Verdict on the Shroud is NOT* an official publication of *The Shroud of Turin Research Project*. While the book is based in part on scientific work done by The Project, the book was not authorized, sponsored or approved in any way by The Project and the conclusions reached by the authors are their own. They do not necessarily represent those of members of the scientific team. All of the names of members of the scientific team should be deleted from the Acknowledgements page.

---

(My copy arrived with the last sentence deleted and the Acknowledgements page cut out.)

Other STURP members have left the fold under different circumstances. Dr. Walter McCrone considers that he was "drummed out" by STURP's refusal to publish his reports (containing the evidence of artists' pigments) and he resigned. An Associated Press story[13] referred to certain unidentified "former members" of the Project who had joined in the lawsuit against Stevenson and Habermas' publisher, although it does not explain why they are no longer on the STURP team. Another defector from Sindondom is Father David Sox, the Episcopal priest and former secretary of the British Society for the Turin Shroud, who resigned from the Society when McCrone's evidence persuaded him the cloth is a probable forgery.

Sox, who served on a committee for carbon-dating the shroud, seems particularly annoyed with Turin's handling of proposals to conduct the carbon-dating tests. Turin vetoed such proposals in 1973 on the grounds that too large a piece of cloth would be required. Actually, two of the small pieces removed by the commission experts are sufficient for several tests (only a fingernail-size piece is now required), and under the repair patches on the shroud is enough additional linen for literally hundreds of dating tests. At the 1978 congress in Turin a carbon-dating expert was present but was not allowed to make a formal presentation. Although the expert had earlier submitted a test proposal to Turin authorities, states Sox, a spokesman for the archbishop "maintained at that time that no formal request for the test had been made."[14] The director of the International Sindonological Center assured the congress participants that the commission samples would be made available when two laboratories were in agreement to conduct the tests. But when that condition was soon met, the Turin spokesman said of the tests:

We do not believe they are accurate enough yet. At present they can only fix the date of an object within a 200-year margin...we believe that the best thing is to wait for ten years until Carbon 14 dating can fix the age of an object with greater accuracy.[15]

(Actually an accuracy of about ± 150 years can now be expected.[16])

Why are Turin authorities reluctant to allow the cloth to be dated? As Dr. Mueller explains:

Any replicated date more recent than about A.D. 300 would establish that it is not the burial cloth of Christ. However, since an artist might well have bothered to obtain ancient linen, a date of even A.D. 30 ±100 could not rule out forgery. Hence, the church hierarchy has little incentive, and considerable disincentive (unless its faith in the shroud is very strong), to permit radiocarbon dating.[17]

In the meantime, despite the evidence for artifice, one can expect sindonologists to continue to promote their views. They are still enjoying willing assistance from the media. For example, ABC's "20/20" has twice aired an Easter program on the shroud that omits the skeptical evidence (for example, the reported confession of the forger and the evidence of artists' pigments) and gives the impression that the shroud is authentic. A leading STURP scientist on the show asserted: "The likelihood of this being a forgery is less than one in ten million, in my opinion."

But there are a few good signs. One, hopefully, is the formation of our critical-review team, whose experts intend to continue to monitor the shroud investigation. Although we have been refused permission to conduct our own examination, there is always the possibility that that will change. And we are prepared to participate actively in arrangements for carbon dating—should it be allowed—to help assure that it is as fair and impartial as possible.

Professor Curtis MacDougall, the distinguished former professor of journalism at Northwestern University, is writing a book on "how the press promotes ignorance and superstition." The press can certainly expect criticism for its largely one-sided coverage of the shroud investigation and accompanying brouhaha.

We hope an editorial in the *New York Times*[18] may herald a new direction for the press. The editorial briefly presented some of the evidence against the shroud's authenticity and concluded: "We excel over our medieval forebears in many things, no doubt, but should try not to outdo them in credulity."

# Appendix

## A Summary Critique of Analyses
## of the "Blood" on the Turin "Shroud"

Scientific tests of the so-called "bloodstains" on the cloth of Turin began in 1973, when experts from an official commission excised several threads and subjected them to forensic analyses. All the tests were negative (see Chapter 12). Subsequently, Dr. Walter C. McCrone, the noted American microanalyst, examined 32 sticky-tape samples that were lifted from the cloth in 1978. On the basis of light and polarized-light microscopy, chemical tests, and sophisticated instrumental analyses, he subsequently reported the identification of artists' materials on the shroud image. Specifically, he identified on the "body" image (sparsely) and "blood" areas (abundantly) particles of iron oxide, which he found to be identical in properties to an artist's pigment. In a "blood"-area tape he detected further a significant amount of artist's vermilion and traces of rose madder, plus a proteinaceous material which, after optical and chemical analyses, he concluded was collagen tempera (a painting medium used in the Middle Ages). On the basis of these findings Dr. McCrone stated that the shroud was probably produced by an artist in the fourteenth century (see Chapters 11 and 12).

Other scientists on the Shroud of Turin Research Project (STURP) had carried out X-ray fluorescence measurements on the shroud in 1978. They detected calcium, iron, and strontium, with calcium being found in the greatest quantity. Iron was detected in greater amounts in "blood" areas than in non-"blood" areas.[1]

In sharp contrast to the findings of the commission scientists and the

_Note: The Appendix was written by_ JOHN F. FISCHER, _with the assistance of Joe Nickell and Dr. Marvin M. Mueller._

McCrone laboratories, STURP's Samuel Pellicori concluded, "There is sufficient correlation in the spectrophotometry to decide that the material on the Shroud is blood."[2] We find such a conclusion to be highly questionable. Pellicori used reflectance spectroscopy, which gave much less contrast than desirable. He therefore converted the reflectance data to absorption data, attempting to correct it by using Kubelka-Monk theory. But the resulting spectrum is also "distorted,"[3] and as Fiori observes, "Recording of absorption spectra without performing chemical reactions is open in any case to serious errors." He adds:

> Although it is certainly true that under identical conditions the same substances have identical absorption spectra, spectra which are apparently identical are insufficient evidence for chemical identity. It is always necessary to demonstrate identical changes in spectra when chemical reactions are performed before the identity of two substances may be assumed.[4]

STURP scientists John Heller and Alan Adler conducted further tests. They first received only a single tape sample from the shroud, which they microscopically examined and then conducted visible light microspectrophotometry. They admitted their "identification is much less positive than desired."[5]

They continued their examination by fuming the *entire* tape sample with 97% hydrazine, followed by fuming with 97% formic acid. Subsequent irradiation with long-wave ultraviolet light produced a red fluorescent spot, which they interpreted as indicative of porphyrin species. By treating the tape with hydrazine and formic acid, they severely etched the tape and were therefore unable to provide a final microspectrophotometric confirmation for the identity of blood. Since many kinds of porphyrins are present in common plant and animal substances, even a fragment of a leaf, for example, could produce similar fluorescence.[6] Most interesting in this regard is the fact that a trace of rose madder pigment (identified by McCrone) — bound in a matrix of a red-ochre collagen tempera paint — can give a similar result. Thus, not only is Heller and Adler's early claim to have "identified the presence of blood" unwarranted but their results could equally be interpreted to support McCrone's determination that there were traces of rose madder in the "blood" areas of the shroud.

More recently, Heller and Adler conducted much more extensive examinations on the tape samples obtained from McCrone. Their report[7] is lengthy (and perhaps necessarily vague in places), but we will briefly address the new findings.

They did positively detect a single particle of artist's vermilion, which seems supportive of McCrone's findings although it does not agree with the quantity he reported. The lesser amount of vermilion may be attributable to McCrone's sophisticated instrumentation being much more capable of detecting the vermilion particles (among the similarly birefringent iron oxide ones) than was conventional light microscopic or polarized-light microscopic examination, as McCrone himself found. We believe that Heller and Adler gave insufficient weight to McCrone's findings (as in the instance of the rose madder). We did give serious consideration to the possibility of artists' pigments being present in the "blood," as was mentioned in Chapter 12.

One of Heller and Adler's new tests was for "heme breakdown products, that is, bile pigments such as bilirubin," and from their positive results they attempt to explain the exceptional red color of the "blood" as due to resulting porphyrin rings. But surely the burden is on them to go beyond mere conjecture in this regard and produce a similarly ancient (600- to 2000-year-old) blood stain that is red in color. The problem here is magnified by the reported presence of crystalline $Fe_2O_3$, vermilion, and madder. This aside, even if one concedes that their results were not due to false-positive-reaction-giving substances, and that bilirubin is indeed present, there is a plausible explanation consistent with the earlier findings of the Commission scientists and Walter McCrone: As indicated in Chapter 12, "Lombard gold" could have been used in a vermilion tempera and, following Heller and Adler's test procedure, we obtained similar results with this pigment—both alone and in combination with various substances previously identified on the shroud.

The two scientists have challenged McCrone's amido-black test, which indicated proteinaceous material; instead they utilized other tests on the basis of which they report the presence of protein, specifically albumin. Thus the argument here concerns a proteinaceous artist's medium versus a protein found in blood. Several things need to be said in this regard. Heller and Adler object to amido black on the grounds that it stains pure cellulose fibers as well as proteinaceous material. However, McCrone specifically used non-image-bearing fibers as controls, and his published color photomicrographs clearly show very minimal fibril staining in contrast to the agglomerates which have stained a very deep blue.

Regarding the protein tests Heller and Adler used, all will react positively for collagen but only one is considered selective for albumin. Even with conclusive proof of the presence of albumin, however, one should not rush to presume the identification of *serum* albumin,[8] since egg tempera contains albumin in copious amounts. Still more unfortunate for the case they are trying to make, the Bromcresol Green test for albumin is critically pH dependent.[9] Recalling the large amounts of calcium rather uniformly distributed on the shroud, we tested linen samples treated with certain calcium compounds (for example, lime, which was used in ancient times to bleach linen[10]) and obtained positive reactions for "albumin," although *none was present.*

Heller and Adler conducted two further tests for blood substances, one using hydrazine to dissolve the "blood"-like material. They report thereby obtaining a "pink hemochromagen-like color"; however, we obtained similar visual results using tempera paint composed of the pigments and medium identified by McCrone. Their second test utilized ammonium hydroxide and potassium cyanide, which they reported gave a "characteristic cyanmethemoglobin type color." Here again results were obtained with tempera paint that fall within the expected color range. However, such visual subjectivity is not adequate for these tests without the performance of confirmatory spectrophotometic analyses.[11]

Finally, whereas McCrone reports only various hydrated oxide forms of iron on the shroud, Heller and Adler mention observing several different ferruginous forms: cellulosic-bound iron (detectible without acid digestion), birefringent "red particles" which "appear to be $Fe_2O_3$," and "orange and brown globs" and "red shards," which require acid digestion for testing. Now, there are many types of ferric oxide pigment. Using the medieval method described by Theophilus[12]—which produces iron oxide pigment by the calcination of ferrous sulfate (green vitriol)—we determined by experimentation that even after repeated washings this iron oxide pigment may still contain significant amounts of residual iron salts. Microscopic and microchemical tests on collagen tempera made with this particular iron pigment give results apparently consistent with those reported by the two STURP scientists.

In summarizing Heller and Adler's report on their investigation of the "blood" stains on the cloth of Turin, we find many of their tests questionable, and we observe that tempera paint could produce similar results. We further note that they did not conduct a single test that was specific for blood. We therefore take strong exception to their conclusion that "the presence of whole blood was established."

# Notes

## Preface

1. Rupert Furneaux, *The World's Most Intriguing True Mysteries* (New York: Arco Publishing Co., 1969), 191.
2. See Chapter 5.
3. The shroud measures approximately 4.3 x 1.1 meters.
4. Yves Delage, in a letter to *Revue Scientifique,* quoted in Thomas Humber, *The Sacred Shroud* (New York: Pocket Books, 1978), 126. See Chapter 7 for a discussion of Delage's involvement with the shroud.
5. Peter M. Rinaldi, *It Is the Lord* (New York: Warner Books, 1973), 7.
6. Joe Nickell, "The Shroud of Turin—Solved," *The Humanist* 38 (Nov./Dec. 1978), 30–32.
7. Marvin M. Mueller, "The Shroud of Turin: A Critical Appraisal," *The Skeptical Inquirer* 6, no. 3 (Spring 1982), 15. (*The Skeptical Inquirer* is the official journal of the Committee for the Scientific Investigation of Claims of the Paranormal, 1203 Kensington Ave., Buffalo, N.Y. 14215. Fellows of the Committee include such distinguished scientists as Isaac Asimov and Carl Sagan.)
8. José Ortega y Gasset, in one of his early books, *Meditations on Quixote*.

## Chapter 1: The Scandal at Lirey

1. Paul Vignon, *The Shroud of Christ*, trans. from the French, 1902 (New York: University Books, 1970), 53 ff.
2. Ian Wilson, *The Shroud of Turin,* rev. ed. (Garden City, N.Y.: Image Books, 1979), 193.
3. H. David Sox, *File on the Shroud* (London: Coronet Books, 1978), 39. Cf. R. W. Hynek, *The True Likeness* (New York: Sheed & Ward, 1951), 9.
4. Wilson, 259.
5. M. de Mély in *La Revue Critique* (Dec. 24–31, 1900), cited by Vignon, 54.
6. Vignon, 54. The date, 1355, is suggested by the d'Arcis letter (see note 9),

---

*Note: Full publishing information (place, publisher, date) is supplied only in the first citation of a work.*

written in 1389, which says the shroud was exhibited 34 years earlier "or thereabouts."

7. Rinaldi, *It Is the Lord,* 16. Cf. *The Catholic Encyclopedia* (1913): "Troyes, Diocese of," Vol. 15, p. 67. This is supported by d'Arcis' letter.

8. Wilson, 194; Sox, 41.

9. Pierre d'Arcis, draft of a memorandum to Pope Clement VII, 1389. This document is in the Collection de Champagne, Bibliothéque Nationale (Paris), Vol. 154, folio 138. The English translation of the Latin original was made by the Rev. Herbert Thurston and published in "The Holy Shroud and the Verdict of History," *The Month,* CI (1903), 17–29. This translation is given in its entirety in an appendix in Wilson, 266–272.

10. Werner Bulst, *The Shroud of Turin* (Milwaukee: Bruce, 1957), 9.

11. D'Arcis in Wilson, 268.

12. Ibid., 269.

13. Edward A. Wuenschel, *Self-Portrait of Christ: The Holy Shroud of Turin* (Esopus, N.Y.: Holy Shroud Guild, 1957), 64; John Walsh, *The Shroud* (New York: Random House, 1963), 53.

14. Walsh, 54.

15. Wilson, 205–206.

16. D'Arcis in Wilson, 269.

17. Thomas Humber, *The Sacred Shroud* (New York: Pocket Books, 1978), 96.

18. See for example Wilson, 207-210; Vignon, 54.

19. Wilson, 87.

20. Sox, 39. See also Vignon, 53.

21. Humber, 100; Wuenschel, 64; Bulst, 14.

22. Walsh, 56; Humber, 100.

23. In Cyr Ulysse Chevalier, *Etude critique sur l'origine du Saint Suaire de Lirey-Chambéry-Turin* (Paris, 1900), quoted in English trans. by Wilson, 212.

24. Humber, 101; Wilson, 212-213, 260-261.

25. Wilson, 212.

26. Humber, 104.

27. Humber, 102 Wilson (214) spells the chronicler's name "Zantiflet."

28. Quoted in Wilson, 214; see also Humber, 102.

29. Wilson, 214.

30. Humber, 103; Wilson, 214, 261; Sox, 43.

31. Sox, 42-43. Sox rightly says the account is "surely apocryphal" and comes from the 16th-century historian, Pignone.

32. Humber, 103. Wilson (261) gives the year as 1459.

33. Humber, 103-104.

34. Wilson, 261. Humber (104) gives the year as 1359.

35. Humber, 104.

36. Or possibly 1482; "the date is uncertain," says Humber, 104.

37. Walsh, 51. ("The Peculiar Affair at Lirey" is Chap. 5 of Walsh's book.)

38. Humber, 113.

39. Chevalier, 1900, quoted in Humber, 106.

## Chapter 2: From Chambéry to Turin

1. Wilson, *The Shroud of Turin,* 215. (Apart from information concerning the shroud, for which I have relied heavily on Wilson, data on the Savoys comes from standard reference sources.)

2. *Encyclopaedia Britannica,* 1960, Vol. 20, p. 26.

3. Quoted in Wilson, 217.

4. Wilson, 216.

5. Wilson, 262.

6. Hynek, *The True Likeness,* 11; cf. Wilson, 25. Hynek states the shroud was exhibited at Lierre.

7. Wilson, 218.

8. Pierre Barbet, *A Doctor at Calvary,* Fr. ed., 1950; Eng. trans. (Garden City, N.Y.: Image Books, 1963), 9.

9. Wilson, 219.

10. Hynek, 11. He gives the date as "the night of December 3," but Wilson (262) and others state December 4.

11. Wilson, 24.

12. Vignon, *The Shroud of Christ,* 77-78; Wilson, 219.

13. Vignon, 78; cf. Wilson, 24; Barbet, 8. During the 1978 investigation, the back of the cloth was partially exposed and it was noted that only the "blood" stains penetrate the cloth.

14. Humber, *The Sacred Shroud,* 179.

15. Wilson, 219, 263.

16. Wilson, 220, 263.

17. Ibid. Cf. Sox, *File on the Shroud* 44-45; Humber, 105.

18. Robert K. Wilcox, *Shroud* (New York: Macmillan, 1977), 18; see also Wilson, 265.

19. Wilson, 216, 264.

20. Quoted in Wilson, 221.

21. Hynek, 11; Wilson, 264.

22. Humber, 28.

23. Humber, 25-33.

24. Humber, 116 ff. The pair were Paul Vignon and Yves Delage.

25. See *Proceedings of the 1977 United States Conference of Research on the Shroud of Turin* (Bronx, N.Y.: Holy Shroud Guild, 1977), 219-220.

26. Wilcox, 44.

27. Humber, 179.

## Chapter 3: The Jewish Burial of Jesus

1. The painting is reproduced in Kenneth E. Weaver, "The Mystery of the Shroud," *National Geographic* 157 (June 1980), 730.

2. Kenneth E. Stevenson and Gary R. Habermas, *Verdict on the Shroud* (Ann Arbor, Mich.: Servant Books, 1981), 43.

3. Isaac Asimov, *Asimov's Guide to the Bible,* Vol. 2 (New York: Equinox Books, 1969), 108.

4. Asimov, 108-109. This view is the one generally held by New Testament scholars.

5. Stevenson and Habermas, 48; see also Humber, *The Sacred Shroud,* 64-65; Wilson, *The Shroud of Turin,* 57.

6. Barbet, *Doctor at Calvary* 162-163; Wilson, 57; Humber, 65.

7. Barbet, 163.

8. Wilcox, *Shroud,* 60-62.

9. Ibid.

10. Rev. J. R. Dummelow, ed., *A Commentary on the Holy Bible by Various Writers* (New York: Macmillan Co., 1951), 808. See also Josh McDowell and Don Stewart, *Answers to Tough Questions Skeptics Ask About the Christian Faith* (San Bernardino, Ca.: Here's Life Publishers, Inc., 1980), 165-166.

11. See Wilson, 57-58, for a contrary view. See also John A. T. Robinson, "The Shroud of Turin and the Grave-Clothes of the Gospels," *Proceedings of the 1977 United States Conference of Research on the Shroud of Turin* (Bronx, N.Y.: Holy Shroud Guild, 1977), 23-30.

12. Humber, 67 ff.

13. Barbet, 161. He also suggests (171) that Lazarus was wrapped in a *sindon,* with "bandlets" being used to hold the legs together and bind the arms to the body.

14. Humber, 70.

15. Humber, 62-63.

16. Dummelow, 771-772; see also Asimov, 290-298.

17. McDowell and Stewart, 165-166.

18. Barbet, 172.

19. Robinson, 27.

20. Rev. Bernard Orchard, OSB, Ealing Abbey, London; quoted in Sox, 157, note 4.

21. L. A. Schwalbe and R. N. Rogers, "Physics and Chemistry of the Shroud of Turin: A Summary of the 1978 Investigation," *Analytica Chimica Acta* 135 (1982), 24.

22. McDowell and Stewart, 166.

23. See Wilson, 93-4, 160.

24. Wilson, 70.

25. Stevenson and Habermas, 62.

26. Joseph and Frances Gies, *Life in a Medieval City,* 1969; reprinted (New York: Harper Colophon Books, 1981), 103, 211-228.

27. Wilson, 70.

28. Gies, 217. According to the editors of *American Fabrics Magazine,* "Until the end of the 14th Century, Egyptian flax was exported to all parts of the commercial world." (*Encyclopedia of Textiles,* 2nd ed., Englewood Cliffs, N.J.: Prentice-Hall, 1972, 142.)

29. Quoted in David F. Brown, "Interview with H. David Sox," *New Realities,* 4, no. 1 (1981), 31. Wilson (69) cites silk examples thought to be Syrian dating from the mid-to-late third century and found at Palmyra and in England.

30. Humber, 35.

31. Wilson, 21.

32. See note 29.

33. Wilson, 13.

34. Wilson, 70-72.

35. Humber, 62.

36. Wilson, 56.

37. McDowell and Stewart, 167.

38. Ibid. (Mish. Shabb. 33:5, from the *Jewish Quarterly Review,* 1895, Vol. 7, p. 118.)

39. Dummelow, 719. Cf. Humber, 65-66.

40. Wilson, 57.

41. Giulio Ricci, "Historical, Medical and Physical Study of the Holy Shroud," *Proceedings,* 58-59. See Stevenson and Habermas on the *Code of Jewish Law,* 46.

42. See Stevenson and Habermas, 27-28; Francis L. Filas, letter, *Industrial Research & Development* (April 1980), 192.

43. See note 29.

44. Mueller, "The Shroud of Turin: A Critical Appraisal," 24.

45. McDowell and Stewart, 168-169.

## Chapter 4: Self-Portraits of Christ?

1. Stevenson and Habermas, *Verdict on the Shroud,* 15.

2. Ibid.

3. Wilson, *The Shroud of Turin,* 98.

4. St. Augustine, *De Trinitate,* Vol. 8, 4, 5, quoted in Wilson, 101.

5. Sox, *File on the Shroud,* 51. See also Wilson, 100. The fresco is in the ancient Syrian town of Dura-Europos on the Euphrates River.

6. Marcello Craveri, *The Life of Jesus,* 1966; reprinted in trans. (New York: Grove Press, 1967), 163.

7. Humber, *The Sacred Shroud,* 83; Wilson, 112.

8. Humber, 84. See note 21.

9. The text of Abgar's reputed "letter" to Jesus was included in an "official history" of the Edessan Image written "shortly after the cloth's translation to Constantinople from Edessa," according to Wilson. This "history" is given in translation in Wilson, 272-290, and I have used it as my primary source for details of the Abgar legend.

10. Ibid.

11. Ibid.

12. Ibid.

13. Sir Steven Runciman, in an article on the Edessan Image in the *Cambridge Historical Journal,* quoted in Sox, 52.

14. Wilson, 106 ff.

15. *Encyclopaedia Britannica,* 1960, Vol. 23, p. 90A. For other versions, see *New Catholic Encyclopedia,* 1967, Vol. 14, p. 625.

16. Ibid.

17. From Juliana of Norwich's *Revelations,* quoted in Wilson, 108.

18. Humber, 85.

19. Eusebius, *Historia Ecclesiastica,* i, 13; vii, 18. (See note 15; Wilson, 110-111, 127-128, 253; Humber, 84.) *New Catholic Encyclopedia,* 1967, Vol. 14, p. 625.

20. See note 19.

21. *The Doctrine of Addai the Apostle,* trans. by Phillips and Wright, and quoted in Wilson, 130. (The manuscript is preserved in Leningrad.)

22. See note 9.

23. For example, this is the title of Edward A. Wuenschel's *Self-Portrait of Christ: The Holy Shroud of Turin* (see note 13, Chapter 1).

24. See illustration in Wilson, following page 192.

25. See note 9.

26. Wilson, 115.

27. Wilpert in Wilson, 107.

28. Wilson, 107.

29. Ibid.

30. Humber, 92.

31. My own experiments show this is possible. For recognizable—if deformed— images of this type, see Vignon, *The Shroud of Christ,* illustration following page 132. See also Nickell, "The Shroud of Turin—Unmasked," *The Humanist* 38, no. 1 (Jan./Feb. 1978), 20-22.

32. Wilson, 116.

33. Wilson, 115.

34. Wilson, 119-121.

35. Wilson, 119, 139, 155, 253-257.

36. Runciman in Sox, 55.

37. Sox, 55-56.

38. Quoted in trans. in Wilson, 108, 115, 158.

39. Ibid., 159.

## Chapter 5: The Shroud as a "Relic"

1. "Relics," *New Catholic Encyclopedia,* 1967, Vol. 12, p. 234.

2. Ibid. A possible exception is Exodus 13:19; however, the *New Catholic Encyclopedia* states it is "vain to seek a justification for the cult of relics in the Old Testament."

3. Ibid.

4. I Infancy 2:2 in *The Lost Books of the Bible and the Forgotten Books of Eden* (New York: William Collins & World Publ. Co., 1976).

5. I Infancy 4:16; 13:16-20; 3:8.

6. Barbara W. Tuchman, *A Distant Mirror: The Calamitous 14th Century* (New York: Ballantine Books, 1978), 237.

7. "Relics," *New Catholic Encyclopedia,* 235.

8. St. Augustine, quoted in "Relics," *Encyclopaedia Britannica,* 1973. See also Karl E. Meyer, "Were You There When They Photographed My Lord?" *Esquire* (August 1971), 73.

9. "Relics," *New Catholic Encyclopedia,* 235.

10. Meyer, 73.

11. Dr. Howard W. Haggard, *Devils, Drugs and Doctors* (New York: Harper & Row, 1929), 301. In addition to Haggard I have relied on the following sources for information on specific relics: E. Cobham Brewer, *A Dictionary of Miracles* (Philadelphia: J. B. Lippincott, 1884), 257-268; Meyer, 73; "Riches Revealed," *Time* (Dec. 29, 1976), 44 ff.; Craveri (see note 6, Chapter 4), 60; Lloyd M. Graham, *Deceptions and Myths of the Bible* (New York: Bell, 1979), 471; Avro Manhattan, *The Vatican Billions* (London: Paravision Books, 1972), 22-23. (See also note 19.)

12. Brewer, 261-262.

13. Haggard, 301.

14. Meyer, 73.

15. See John 19:29.

16. Craveri, *The Life of Jesus,* 424.

17. Here, as elsewhere in the following discussion of the various reputed burial garments of Jesus, I have relied mainly on Humber, *The Sacred Shroud,* 74-82, and Wilson, *The Shroud of Turin,* 92 ff.

18. Nicholas Mesarites, the patriarch of Constantinople. Quoted in translation in Humber, 78.

19. Robert de Clari, *The Conquest of Constantinople,* trans. from Old French by Edgar Holmes McNeal (New York: Columbia University Press, 1936), 112.

20. Vignon, *The Shroud of Christ,* 55; Wilson, 169.

21. McNeal (see note 19); see also Vignon, 54.

22. Humber, 79; cf. Wilson, 169.

23. Humber, 79.

24. Wilson, 160.

25. Sox quoted in Brown (see note 29, Chapter 3), 34.

26. See Wilson, 109.

27. Sox, *File on the Shroud,* 57; Wilson, 160-161.

28. Wilson, 201-202.

## Chapter 6: Post-mortem at Calvary?

1. Barbet, *A Doctor at Calvary,* 18.

2. For a brief history of the evolving "medical" views on the shroud, see Wilson, *The Shroud of Turin,* 32 ff.

3. Wilcox, *Shroud,* 23.

4. Barbet, from the Preface, x.

5. Dr. Anthony Sava, "The Holy Shroud on Trial," *Proceedings on the 1977 United States Conference of Research on the Shroud of Turin* (Bronx, N.Y.: Holy Shroud Guild, 1977), 54.

6. Sava, 51.

7. Cullen Murphy, "Shreds of Evidence," *Harper's* 263 (November 1981), 44.

8. Dr. Bucklin has published at least one article, "The Legal and Medical Aspects of the Trial and Death of Christ," *Medicine, Science and the Law* 10, no. 1 (January 1970), 14-26.

9. For example, in Richard Lewis, "Examination of Turin Shroud Provides Crucifixion Details," *American Medical News* 21 (April 13, 1979).

10. Ibid.

11. Reginald W. Rhein, Jr., "The Shroud of Turin: Medical Examiners Disagree," *Medical World News* 21, no. 26 (December 22, 1980), 40.

12. Quoted in Rhein, 49.

13. Rhein, 49-50.

14. Humber, *The Sacred Shroud,* 137. Illustrations of two different models of the *flagrum* are given in Wilcox, 33.

15. Barbet, p. 92.

16. Rinaldi, *It Is the Lord* (see note 7, Chapter 1), 28.

17. Wuenschel, *Self-Portrait of Christ: The Holy Shroud of Turin* (see note 13, Chapter 1), 49.

18. *Proceedings*, 58-73. (The quote is from page 60.)

19. Wuenschel, 50.

20. Ambrose Bierce, *The Devil's Dictionary*, 1910 (New York: Castle Books, 1967), n.p.

21. Ricci, *Proceedings* (see note 41, Chapter 3), 64.

22. Barbet, 91-92

23. Bernard S. Myers, ed., *McGraw-Hill Dictionary of Art* (New York: McGraw-Hill, 1969), 407.

24. See for example, Joan Evans, *Life in Medieval France,* 3rd ed. (London: Phaidon, 1969), plate 81: "A Procession of Flagellants" (14th century). Wilson, 48, cites the accounts mentioning the *flagrum*.

25. Tuchman, *A Distant Mirror* (see note 6, Chapter 5), 114.

26. Baden in Rhein, 50.

27. Barbet, 93-94. See also, for example, Wilson, 37.

28. Ricci in Wilcox, 47.

29. I gave evidence of this fact in my article in *Christian Life* (Feb. 1980, 23), and it is conceded by Stevenson and Habermas, *Verdict on the Shroud* (40), who state: "An occasional artist depicted the crown as a total covering, but such a style was rare before a time when the Shroud was already known."

30. Baden in Rhein, 50; Sox, *File on the Shroud*, 97 (quoting Peter Freeland).

31. Stevenson and Habermas, 38.

32. Sava, 55.

33. Sava, 56. Cf. Barbet, 109-110.

34. Humber, 153-157.

35. Craveri, *The Life of Jesus,* 413; see also Barbet, 42.

36. Dr. Marvin Mueller, personal communication (reporting on a local late-September 1980 STURP talk he attended), dated October 4, 1980.

37. Vignon, *The Shroud of Christ*, 78.

38. Marcel Blanc (in a debate with Michel de Boüard), "Le suaire de Turin est-il le linceul du Christ?" *L'Histoire* (February 20, 1980), 112; personal communication, Paris, February 3, 1980.

39. Zugibe in Rhein, 48.

40. Barbet, 118-119; see also Humber, 141.

41. *Proceedings,* 199-201.

42. Barbet, 122.

43. Wilson, 300.

44. Erwin Panofsky, *Early Netherlandish Painting* (Cambridge: Harvard University Press, 1953), 364-365.

45. See, for example, H. W. Janson, *History of Art* (Englewood Cliffs, N.J.: Prentice-Hall, 1963), 254, illustration 405, for a 13th-century example of the crossed-feet, "three-nail-type." See also Sox, 73, and Craveri, 414, for a discussion.

46. For an example, see John Taylor, *Icon Painting* (New York: Mayflower Books, 1979), 10. This painting depicts the feet as nailed separately.

47. Wilson, 50. See the illustration following page 128: "Reconstruction of probable manner of Jehohanan's crucifixion."

48. Vignon, 150. (For other postulated rolls of linen, see page 48.)

49. This "wound" appears on the figure's left side on the shroud, but of course the image is—or is intended to suggest—an imprint. Therefore the wound would have been in the *right* side of the supposed "man in the shroud." It would have been simple for an artist to have imagined this; he need not have thought in terms of photographic reversal at all.

50. See Taylor, 73, for a 14th-century Venetian example.

51. As in the example given in note 50.

52. Zugibe in Rhein, 48.

53. Barbet, 144.

54. See, for example, Giovanni da Milano's "Pieta" (1365) in Janson, 274.

55. Barbet, 140

56. Sava, 52-53; Bucklin (following Willis in this regard) in Rhein, 46.

57. For ultraviolet fluorescence photographs showing the enhanced "auras," see Kenneth F. Weaver, "The Mystery of the Shroud" (see note 1, Chapter 3), 744-746.

58. Ricci, *Proceedings,* 71.

59. Baden in Rhein, 50.

60. Humber, 142.

61. For an example see the monochrome painting on silk in the Louvre, "Parement de Narbonne," plate 384 in the *Encyclopedia of World Art,* Vol. 6 (New York: McGraw-Hill, 1962). This painting is dated 1364-80. (See also Vignon, 32.).

62. Wilcox, 45.

63. This will be discussed in Chapter 12 and the Appendix.

64. Wilcox, 70.

65. Rhein, 50.

66. Stevenson and Habermas, 135-136.

67. Rinaldi, *It Is the Lord*, caption for Figure 8.

68. Rhein, 50.

69. Bucklin in Rhein, 50.
70. Bucklin in Lewis (see note 9).
71. See Janson, *History of Art* (note 45), 273.
72. Rinaldi, caption to Figure 9.
73. Stevenson and Habermas, 134.
74. Barbet, 135.
75. Ibid.
76. Ricci, *Proceedings,* 72.
77. Wilson, 22.
78. Vignon, 131.
79. Vignon, 140.
80. See Ricci, *Proceedings*, 72.
81. Humber, 136.
82. Bucklin, "Legal and Medical Aspects..." (see note 8), 25.
83. Baden in Rhein, 50.
84. Wilcox, 3.
85. Blanc, personal communication (see note 38).
86. Vignon, 140.
87. "Shroud Reveals Lincolnesque Disease," *New Orleans Times-Picayune* (January 31, 1982).
88. Craveri, 165.
89. Carleton S. Coon, quoted in Wilcox, 136.
90. Coon in Ivan T. Sanderson, "The Missing Link," *Argosy* (May 1969), 29.
91. C. Eugene Emery, Jr., "Sasquatchsickle: The Monster, the Model and the Myth," *The Skeptical Inquirer* 6, no. 2 (Winter 1981-82), 2-4; Jerome Clark, "The Iceman Goeth," *Fate* (March 1982) 56-59. (I once saw this fake at a carnival—and recognized it for what it was.)
92. Sox, 70.
93. Sox, 73.
94. *A Sculptor Interprets the Holy Shroud of Turin* (Esopus, N.Y.: Holy Shroud Guild, 1954), 15-17. Although published anonymously, this pamphlet was written by Rev. Weyland (see Wilcox, 161). See also Wilcox, 22-24, 41.
95. Barbet, 15. (Zugibe was quoted in the news article cited in note 87.)
96. Wilson, 35; Weyland (see note 94), 17.
97. Stevenson and Habermas, 35.
98. Wilson, 49-50.
99. Alfred Louis Kroeber, *Anthropology* (New York: Harcourt, Brace & World, 1948), 126-7, 132.
100. Ferri argued similarly. See "How Big Was Jesus Christ?" *Time* (May 15, 1950), cited in Wilcox, 23.
101. Wilson, 45.
102. Rinaldi, 89.
103. Rinaldi, 89-90.
104. Rinaldi, 90.
105. Bucklin in Lewis (see note 9).

106. Zugibe in Rhein, 49.
107. See note 87.
108. Baden in Rhein, 50.
109. Rhein, 40.

## Chapter 7: Contact Prints and Vapor "Photos"

1. Rinaldi, *It Is the Lord*, 25-26.
2. Michael Thomas, "The First Polaroid in Palestine," *Rolling Stone* (December 28, 1978).
3. For a discussion, see Chapter 9.
4. Murphy, "Shreds of Evidence" (see note 7, Chapter 6), 56.
5. Leo Valla, quoted in Wilcox, *Shroud*, 131.
6. Rogers in *Proceedings*, 132-133.
7. Eric Jumper, John Jackson, and Don Devan, in *Proceedings*, 215.
8. Vignon, *The Shroud of Christ*, 129-130.
9. Ricci, in *Proceedings*, 72.
10. Mueller, "The Shroud of Turin" (see note 7, Preface), 27; Murphy, 60.
11. For a discussion, see L. A. Schwalbe and R. N. Rogers, "Physics and Chemistry of the Shroud of Turin" (see note 21, Chapter 3), 33-35. See also Jumper et al. in *Proceedings*, 82-83, 186-187; Stevenson and Habermas, *Verdict on the Shroud*, 194 ff.
12. Vignon, 128.
13. Vignon, 131.
14. Vignon, 132. See photographs between pages 132 and 133.
15. Vignon, 133.
16. See Wueschel's pamphlet, *The Holy Shroud*, 20. Cf. Vignon, 48.
17. Nickell, "The Turin Shroud—Unmasked" (see note 31, Chapter 4), 20-22.
18. Samuel F. Pellicori, "Spectral Properties of the Shroud of Turin," *Applied Optics* 19 (1980), 1917.
19. Ibid.
20. Mueller, 28.
21. Samuel F. Pellicori with Mark S. Evans, "The Shroud of Turin Through the Microscope," *Archaeology* 34, no. 1 (Jan./Feb. 1981), 42.
22. Schwalbe and Rogers, 29.
23. Mueller, 28. This will be discussed more fully in Chapter 13.
24. Pellicori with Evans, 43.
25. Annette Burden, "Shroud of Mystery," *Science 81* (November 1981), 82.
26. Vignon, 137.
27. Humber, *The Sacred Shroud*, 116.
28. Humber, 116-117.
29. Wilson, 32.
30. *Encyclopaedia Britannica*, 1960, Vol. 7, p. 148.
31. Humber, 125.
32. Quoted in Humber, 126.
33. Jumper et al. in *Proceedings*, 182.

34. Ibid., 183. See also Schwalbe and Rogers, 11.
35. Jumper et al. in *Proceedings,* 182. (See also note 38).
36. Ibid., 186.
37. Nickell (see note 17), 21.
38. Schwalbe and Rogers, 29. For a discussion see John P. Jackson in *Proceedings,* 223-233.
39. Schwalbe and Rogers, 32.
40. Ibid., 29 ff.
41. Ibid., 35.

## Chapter 8: Resurrection Radiance?

1. This was Lt. Col. P. W. O'Gorman. See Wilcox, *Shroud,* 119.
2. Ibid., 126.
3. Geoffrey Ashe, "What Sort of Picture?" *Sindon,* 1966, 15-19, quoted in Wilcox, 126.
4. Kenneth E. Stevenson, ed., *Proceedings of the 1977 United States Conference of Research on the Shroud of Turin, March 23-24, 1977, Albuquerque, New Mexico, USA* (Bronx, N.Y.: Holy Shroud Guild, 1977).
5. Vignon, *The Shroud of Christ,* 134 ff.
6. See note 4.
7. John P. Jackson, "Color Analysis of the Turin Shroud: A Preliminary Study," *Proceedings,* 190-195.
8. Humber, *The Sacred Shroud,* 200; Stevenson and Habermas, *Verdict on the Shroud,* 92. See also note 9.
9. *Los Alamos Monitor,* March 24, 1978.
10. Barbara J. Culliton, "The Mystery of the Shroud of Turin Challenges 20th-Century Science," *Science* 201 (1978), 235-239.
11. *Proceedings,* 77.
12. Thomas M. McCown, in *Proceedings,* 100.
13. Eric Jumper, John Jackson, and Don Devan, "Computer Related Investigations of the Holy Shroud," *Proceedings,* 208-210.
14. Ibid., 210-211. (See also *Proceedings,* 75.)
15. Wilson, *The Shroud of Turin,* illustration facing page 160.
16. Barbara M. Sullivan, "How in Fact Was Jesus Christ Laid in His Tomb?" *National Review* (July 20, 1973), 785-789.
17. Schwalbe and Rogers (see note 21, Chapter 3), 8.
18. See *Proceedings,* 81.
19. See Stevenson and Habermas, illustration 22.
20. Mueller, "The Shroud of Turin" (see note 7, Preface), 22-23.
21. Stevenson and Habermas, caption to illustrations 15 and 16. See also Mueller, 23.
22. Stevenson and Habermas, 143 ff.
23. Mueller, 22-25.
24. S. F. Pellicori and R. A. Chandos, "Portable Unit Permits UV/Vis Study of 'Shroud,' " *Industrial Research & Development* (February 1981), 188.

25. Schwalbe and Rogers, 27.

26. Stevenson and Habermas, 196.

27. Mueller attended the STURP conference in October 1979 at the Los Alamos National Laboratory, where he observed numerous photomicrographs of shroud-image areas showing this characteristic.

28. See Stevenson and Habermas, illustration 19.

29. Quoted in Murphy (see note 7, Chapter 6), 65.

30. Stevenson and Habermas, 178-179.

31. Ibid., 181.

32. Jerome S. Goldblatt, "The Shroud," *National Review* (April 16, 1982).

## Chapter 9: Medieval Negatives

1. Humber, *The Sacred Shroud*, 16-17.

2. Editors, *Time-Life Library of Photography: The Camera* (New York: Time, Inc., 1971), 134.

3. See Wilson, *The Shroud of Turin*, 156.

4. See Vignon, *The Shroud of Christ*, 117-118.

5. Quoted in Wilcox, *Shroud*, 109.

6. Vignon, 119. Facing this page are photographs—positive and negative—of the portion of the fresco. The painting is attributed to Cimabue (c. 1240–c. 1302).

7. Wilcox, 57.

8. Vignon, 114.

9. Helen Gardner, *Art Through the Ages* (New York: Harcourt, 1959), 211.

10. Quoted in Sox, *The Image on the Shroud*, 54.

11. Walter McCrone in Sox, ibid., 58.

12. See Cennino Cennini's 15th-century text, *The Craftsman's Handbook* (Il Libro dell' Arte), trans. by Daniel V. Thompson (New York: Dover, 1960), 103, 105. See also Sox, *The Image on the Shroud*, 53.

13. Wuenschel, *The Holy Shroud*, 17.

14. A recent attempt (see Sox, *The Image on the Shroud*, illustration facing page 83), although unfinished, looks quite good; however the photo-reversed positive image is not reproduced.

15. See Wilcox, 58-59; also *Proceedings*, 86-87.

16. Walter McCrone, speaking at a 1980 meeting of the British Society for the Turin Shroud. I am indebted to Reginald W. Rhein, Jr., editor of *Medical World News* for a transcript. (Apparently, the artist is the same one—McCrone's friend, Walter Sanford—who made the copy of the shroud negative mentioned in note 13.)

17. See *National Geographic* 157 (June 1980), 742.

18. Schwalbe and Rogers (see note 21, Chapter 3), 11.

19. Ibid., 14, 29, 31.

20. Vignon, 116-117.

21. See Bernard G. Campbell, *Humankind Emerging* (Boston: Little, Brown, 1976), 405, illustrations 19-27.

22. "Printing," *Encyclopaedia Britannica*, 1973.

23. "Printmaking," *Encyclopedia Britannica*, 1973.

24. Nickell, "The Shroud of Turin—Unmasked" (see note 31, Chapter 4), 20.

25. See note 23.

26. John J. Bodor, *Rubbings and Textures: A Graphic Technique* (New York: Reinhold, 1968), 52.

27. For an early discussion, see note 24. See also Nickell, "The Turin Shroud: Fake? Fact? Photograph?" *Popular Photography* (November 1979), 98.

28. See Schwalbe and Rogers, 24. They argue however that "the radiographs show no discontinuity in the cloth areal density." This means little if anything, since "[D]etails of the two body images, the blood stains and the scorch marks are not discernible in the radiographs." See Mottern et al., *Materials Evaluation* (December 1980), 42.

29. *Proceedings,* 182.

30. Vignon, 135, 144-145.

31. Quoted in Murphy (see note 7, Chapter 6), 56.

32. Vignon, 124.

33. See, for example, the 16th-century copy reproduced in *National Geographic* 157 (June 1980), 732. See also the painting done in 1703 and reproduced on the cover of Sox's *The Image on the Shroud.* In Chapter 1 the pilgrim's medallion, c. 1353-57, with images in bold relief, was mentioned.

34. Quoted in Murphy, 65.

35. See *Proceedings,* 219 ff.

36. Mueller, "The Shroud of Turin" (see note 7, Preface) 24-25.

37. Schwalbe and Rogers, 30.

38. For example, see notes 24, 27.

39. See note 22.

40. Cecily Barth Firestein, *Rubbing Craft* (New York: Quick Fox, 1977), 14.

41. Norman R. Eppink, *101 Prints: The History and Techniques of Printmaking* (Norman, Okla.: University of Oklahoma Press, 1971), 198.

42. Ibid.

43. Bodor, 8.

44. Ibid., 7.

45. Steven D. Shafersman, "Science, the Public, and the Shroud of Turin," *The Skeptical Inquirer* 6 (Spring 1982), 51.

46. Wuenschel, *The Holy Shroud,* 17.

47. Stevenson and Habermas, 110.

48. Narrated by Ephrem Zimbalist, Jr., this documentary was produced by the 700 Club and telecast on CBN at various times in late 1980.

### Chapter 10: Scientific Pilgrimages

1. Wilson, *The Shroud of Turin,* 25.

2. Sox, *The Image on the Shroud,* 79.

3. Schwalbe and Rogers (see note 21, Chapter 3), 47, note 7.

4. Sox, *The Image on the Shroud,* 79-80.

5. Sox, *File on the Shroud,* 63.

6. M. de Mély, quoted in Vignon, *The Shroud of Christ,* 108.

7. Vignon, 110. See also Sox, *File on the Shroud,* 63.

8. Robert D. LaRue, Jr., in *Proceedings,* 219-221.

9. Wilcox, *Shroud,* 16; Sox, *File on the Shroud,* 68.

10. Wilcox, 22-23.

11. *Time,* May 15, 1950.

12. Wilcox, 24.

13. Except as otherwise noted, information on the work of the Turin Commission is taken primarily from Wilcox, 17-77; Wilson, 64-81; Sox, *Image on the Shroud,* 84-116; and Humber, *The Sacred Shroud,* 164-181.

14. Cited in Wilcox (without further publication information), 43-44.

15. Wilcox, 44.

16. Wilson, 67.

17. Humber, 179.

18. Wilson, 65.

19. Humber, 196, Wilcox, 167.

20. Wilson, 80.

21. Ibid., 77.

22. Sox, *Image,* 139.

23. Max Frei, *Naturwissenschaftliche Rundshau* 32 (1979), 133. This was translated privately for our team's study by John Fischer and Wayne Morris.

24. Schwalbe and Rogers, 47, note 4.

25. Burden (see note 25, Chapter 7), 79.

26. Schafersman (see note 45, Chapter 9), 40.

27. John Dart, "Scientists Can't Prove or Deny Its Link to Jesus," *Los Angeles Times,* April 18, 1981.

28. UPI, in the *Albuquerque Journal,* April 3, 1981.

29. See the 1977 *Proceedings.*

30. Wilson, 237. Except as otherwise noted, details concerning the 1978 exposition and STURP's activities in Turin are taken primarily from Wilson, 235-244; Murphy (see note 7, Chapter 6), 42-65; Weaver (see note 1, Chapter 3), 734-752; Sox, *File,* 140-142; Sox, *Image,* 8 ff.

31. Sox, *File,* 141.

32. Quoted in the *Los Alamos Monitor,* March 24, 1978.

33. Rinaldi, from the Acknowledgement, *It Is the Lord.*

34. Quoted in Murphy, see note 30.

35. Schafersman, 44.

36. Dr. Walter McCrone, quoted in Susan Struthers, "New Light on Old Shroud," *Industrial Chemical News* 2 (December 1981), 24.

37. Sox, *File,* 139.

38. Ibid., 141.

39. A few of these are reproduced in Weaver (see note 1, Chapter 3), 743, and Stevenson and Habermas, *Verdict on the Shroud,* illustrations 19 and 20.

40. Eric T. Jumper and Robert W. Mottern, "Scientific Investigation of the Shroud of Turin," *Applied Optics* 19 (June 1980), 1911.

41. Sox, *Image,* 61.

42. From the *Los Angeles Times,* reprinted in the *Sentinel Star* (Orlando, Fla.), April 7, 1979.

43. AP, in *The Courier-Journal* (Louisville, Ky.), May 6, 1979.
44. Ibid.
45. *National Enquirer,* June 19, 1979.
46. *The Lexington* (Ky.) *Leader,* November 19, 1979.
47. Sox, *Image,* 15.

## Chapter 11: The Microanalyst and the Shroud

1. Sox, *Image,* 18 ff.
2. Mueller (see note 7, Preface), 29.
3. Struthers (see note 36, Chapter 10), 1.
4. Murphy (see note 7, Chapter 6), 55.
5. Quoted in Henry Clay Ruark, "The Continuing Search...," *Functional Photography* (May/June 1981), 18. Except as noted otherwise, information on McCrone's background is taken from the sources referenced above as well as from the *MAAFS Newsletter* (the official publication of the Mid-Atlantic Association of Forensic Scientists), 9 (June 1981), 1-2. For an account of the Vinland Map affair, see *The Observer,* January 27, 1974.
6. W. C. McCrone et al., *The Particle Atlas,* Vols. 1-5 (Ann Arbor, Mich.: Ann Arbor Science Publishers, 1973-79).
7. Wilson, *The Shroud of Turin,* 242-243.
8. Walter C. McCrone and Christine Skirius, "Light Microscopical Study of the Turin 'Shroud' I," *The Microscope* 28 (1980), 105-113.
9. Ibid., 105. See also Walter C. McCrone, "What We Found on the Turin Shroud and How We Found It," *Functional Photography* (May/June 1981), 19-20, 30.
10. Sox, *Image,* 15.
11. Quoted in Sox, *Image,* 31. Sox states: "It is important to remember that much of the material quoted and alluded to from the STURP newsletter contains exploratory and speculative material" (141).
12. Sox, *Image,* 34.
13. McCrone, quoted from his preliminary draft abstract, in Sox, *Image,* 34-35.
14. Sox, *Image,* 36-38. See also Schwalbe and Rogers (note 21, Chapter 3), 15.
15. R. A. Morris, L. A. Schwalbe and J. R. London, "X-Ray Fluorescence Investigation of the Shroud of Turin," *X-Ray Spectrometry* 9 (1980), 40-47.
16. Schwalbe and Rogers, 17.
17. S. F. Pellicori, "Spectral Properties of the Shroud of Turin," *Applied Optics* 19 (June 15, 1980), 1919.
18. The quote from Vignon was given in the preceding chapter. See Wilson, 21, 115; Humber, 38; Larue in *Proceedings.* The photomicrograph is given in Stevenson and Habermas, illustration 19.
19. McCrone, February 1980 STURP Newsletter (see note 10), quoted in Sox, *Image,* 39.
20. From a transcript of McCrone's September 1980 talk before the British Society for the Turin Shroud, courtesy of Reginald W. Rhein, Jr.

21. See note 7.
22. Ray Rogers, quoted in "Expert Says Turin Shroud Work of 'Artist,' " UPI, in *San Jose Mercury News,* September 20, 1980.
23. Given in Sox, *Image,* 61.
24. Pellicori (see note 17), 1920.
25. Quoted in Struthers, 24.

## Chapter 12: Is the "Blood" Blood?

1. John H. Heller and Alan D. Adler, *Canadian Society Forensic Science Journal* 14 (1981), 81-103.
2. Wilcox, *Shroud,* 45.
3. Sox, *File,* 141.
4. Paul L. Kirk, *Crime Investigation,* 2nd ed. (New York: John Wiley & Sons, 1974), 194-195.
5. S. S. Kind, David Patterson, and G. W. Owen, *Forensic Science* 1 (1972), 27-54. See also "Use of Reflectance Measurements in Assessing the Colour Changes of Ageing Bloodstains," *Nature* 187 (1960), 688-689.
6. Sox, *File,* 93.
7. Kirk, 183; See also Fred E. Inbau, et al., *Scientific Police Investigation* (New York: Chilton Book Co., 1972), 116-117.
8. Wilson, *The Shroud of Turin,* 72-77; Sox, *File,* 92-93. According to Wilson (page 75), Frache's "more specific tests" (for example, for blood-grouping) were negative. As this book goes to press, we have just learned of a recent Italian analysis that supposedly "indicated" the "blood" was "human blood," based on "fluorescent antigen-antibody reactions." (This is cited in an article by W. Meacham to be published in *Current Anthropology.*) Although we lack further details, we can state that Frache's negative results, plus the lack of identification of blood per se, cast grave doubt on whether this test would be valid. The problem is magnified by the age of the stains (at least 600 years old), and by the presence of many foreign substances (which might cause false-positive results).
9. Wilson, 74-75; Sox, *File,* 93.
10. A. Fiori, "Detection and Identification of Bloodstains," in F. Lundquist, ed., *Methods of Forensic Science,* Vol. 1 (New York: Interscience, 1962), 269.
11. Sox, *File,* 93.
12. Quoted in Sox, *File,* 90.
13. Inbau, 130-131.
14. Sox, *File,* 138.
15. Wilson, 263.
16. Theophilus, in a 12th-century text, *On Divers Arts,* trans. by John G. Hawthorne and Cyril Stanley Smith (New York: Dover, 1979), 113; see also Cennini (see note 12, Chapter 9), 25, 79-83, 198 ff.
17. Quoted in Sox, *File,* 138.
18. McCrone and Skirius (see note 8, Chapter 11), 110.
19. See note 20, Chapter 11.

20. Walter C. McCrone, "Miscroscopical Study of the Turin 'Shroud'; III," *The Microscope* 29 (1981), 19-38.

21. McCrone, from an April 22, 1980, communication to STURP, quoted in Sox, *Image,* 63.

22. Cennini, 95. See also Sox, *Image,* 49; Max Doerner, *The Materials of the Artist* (New York: Harcourt, 1949), 72.

23. Theophilus, 14 ff. See also Sox, *Image,* 53.

24. John Glaister, *A Text-Book of Medical Jurisprudence and Toxicology* (New York: William Wood & Co., 1921), 376-378.

25. Walter C. McCrone, "Light Microscopical Study of the Turin 'Shroud' II," *The Microscope* 28 (1980), 115-128.

26. Rutherford J. Gettens and George L. Stout, *Painting Materials: A Short Encyclopaedia,* 1942; reprinted (New York: Dover, 1966), 25-27, 69-71. See also Daniel V. Thompson, *The Materials and Techniques of Medieval Painting,* 1936; reprinted (New York: Dover, 1956), 34, 64-65.

27. Gettens and Stout, 25.

28. S. F. Pellicori, "Spectral Properties of the Shroud of Turin," *Applied Optics* 19 (1980), 1913-1920.

29. John H. Heller and Alan D. Adler, "Blood on the Shroud of Turin," *Applied Optics* 19 (1980), 2742-2744.

30. See note 1.

31. One by Theophilus and another by Cennini (see note 16). See also Thompson, note 26 above.

32. Theophilus, 115. This is discussed in Chapter 13.

33. Thompson, 108.

### Chapter 13: The "Yellow Fibers" Mystery

1. Mueller, "The Shroud of Turin" (see note 7, Preface), 30.

2. Schwalbe and Rogers (see note 21, Chapter 3), 31.

3. Ibid., 11.

4. McCrone, from a lengthy letter "to Turin," quoted in Sox, *Image,* 42.

5. McCrone, from the abstract to his second report in *The Microscope* 28 (1980), 115.

6. See Appendix for discussion.

7. Schwalbe and Rogers, 14.

8. Rogers, quoted in Sox, *Image,* 91. See also Schwalbe and Rogers, 11.

9. Schwalbe and Rogers, 12.

10. Ibid., 14.

11. S. F. Pellicori and R. A. Chandos, "Portable Unit Permits UV/Vis Study of 'Shroud,' " *Industrial Research & Development* (February 1981), 189.

12. Schwalbe and Rogers, 29.

13. Ibid., 29-30.

14. Ibid., 30.

15. Ibid., 28.

16. Mueller, 31-32.

17. We note the importance of photochemical reactions presently. One of Fischer's experiments concerned the "photo" effect of sunlight on bleached linen, as we noted briefly in Chapter 9. He speculated that the shroud image might have been produced by applied paints or pigments on unbleached (yellow) linen. Subsequent explosure to sunlight would bleach the *non-image* areas (as well as the back of the cloth), whereas the fibers covered by the pigment would potentially remain yellow. As the density of the pigment increased, so accordingly would the number of yellow fibers.

18. See Appendix.

19. McCrone, "Microscopical Study of the Turin 'Shroud'; III" (see note 20, Chapter 12), 19-38.

20. Y. P. Kathpalia, *Conservation and Restoration of Archive Materials* (Paris: UNESCO, 1973), 72.

21. Per E. Guldbeck, *The Care of Historical Collections* (Nashville, Tenn.: American Association for State and Local History, 1972), 121.

22. W. Gardner, *Textile Laboratory Manual,* Vol. 3 (New York: American Elsevier, 1967), 140.

23. Editors, *American Fabrics Magazine, Encyclopedia of Textiles* (Englewood Cliffs, N.J.: Prentice-Hall, 1972), 141.

24. G. Shaefer, *Ciba Review* 49 (April 1945), 1762-1777.

25. Ibid., 21; Thompson (see note 26, Chapter 12), 82.

26. Kathpalia, 51.

27. Gettens and Stout (see note 26, Chapter 12), 154.

28. Ibid., 169.

29. Theophilus, 115. (See also the translators' note, page 14.)

30. For this particular use, Theophilus added salt plus wine or urine and ground it to a thick paste.

31. *Chambers's Encyclopaedia*, 1967, Vol. 7, p. 749.

32. R. L. Feller, "The Deteriorating Effect of Light on Museum Objects," *Museum News Technical Supplement,* no. 3 (June 1964).

33. Thompson, 76-77.

34. Sox, *Image,* 97.

35. Schwalbe and Rogers (page 29) cite the suggestion of Druzik, who is not further identified.

## Chapter 14: Summation and Aftermath

1. Schafersman, "Science, the Public, and the Shroud of Turin" (see note 45, Chapter 9), 42.

2. Wilson, *The Shroud of Turin,* 51-53.

3. Stevenson and Habermas, *Verdict on the Shroud,* 121-129.

4. Ibid., 128.

5. Schafersman, 49.

6. *New York Times,* January 28, 1982.

7. For example, in the tabloid, *Globe,* October 27, 1981.

8. Stevenson and Habermas, 183.

9. Mueller (see note 7, Preface), 29.

10. Review by John Dart, reprinted in *The Courier-Journal,* (Louisville, Ky.), December 20, 1981.

11. Schafersman, 52.

12. Stephen C. Smith, "Tests Can't Tell Whether Shroud Was Christ's, Scientists Say," *The Courier-Journal,* October 10, 1980. See also Schafersman, 52-53.

13. Ibid.

14. Sox, *Image,* 130.

15. Quoted in Sox, *Image,* 130.

16. Schwalbe and Rogers (see note 21, Chapter 3), 43.

17. Mueller, 32.

18. *New York Times,* December 4, 1981.

## Appendix

1. R. A. Morris, L. A. Schwalbe and J. R. London (see note 15, Chapter 11), 40-47.

2. S. F. Pellicori (see note 28, Chapter 12), 1913-20.

3. John H. Heller and Alan D. Adler (see note 29, Chapter 12), 2742-44.

4. A. Fiori, "Detection and Identification of Bloodstains," in F. Lundquist, ed., *Methods of Forensic Science,* Vol. 1 (New York: Interscience, 1962).

5. Heller and Adler.

6. John F. Fischer, *The Microscope* 29 (1981), 69-70.

7. John H. Heller and Alan D. Adler, *Canadian Society Forensic Science Journal* 14 (1981), 81-103.

8. F. Fiegel and V. Anger, *Spot Tests in Organic Analysis,* trans. by R. Oesper, (New York: Elsevier, 1975).

9. Ibid. See also W. White, M. Erickson, and S. Stevens, *Chemistry for Medical Technologists* (St. Louis: C. V. Mosby Co., 1970).

10. *Encyclopaedia Britannica,* 1960, Vol. 14, p. 130.

11. Fiori.

12. See Chapter 13 for discussion.

# Index

# PAPERBACKS AVAILABLE FROM PROMETHEUS BOOKS

## SCIENCE AND THE PARANORMAL

____ESP & Parapsychology: A Critical Re-evaluation   *C.E.M. Hansel*   $9.95

____Extra-Terrestrial Intelligence   *James L. Christian, editor*   7.95

____Flim-Flam!   *James Randi*   9.95

____Objections to Astrology   *L. Jerome & B. Bok*   4.95

____The Psychology of the Psychic   *D. Marks & R. Kammann*   9.95

____Philosophy & Parapsychology   *J. Ludwig, editor*   9.95

____Paranormal Borderlands of Science   *Kendrick Frazier, editor*   13.95

____The Truth About Uri Geller   *James Randi*   8.95

## HUMANISM

____Ethics Without God   *K. Nielsen*   6.95

____Humanist Alternative   *Paul Kurtz, editor*   5.95

____Humanist Ethics   *Morris Storer, editor*   9.95

____Humanist Funeral Service   *Corliss Lamont*   3.95

____Humanist Manifestos I & II   1.95

____Humanist Wedding Service   *Corliss Lamont*   2.95

____Humanistic Psychology   *Welch, Tate, Richards, editors*   10.95

____Moral Problems in Contemporary Society   *Paul Kurtz, editor*   7.95

____Secular Humanist Declaration   1.95

____Voice in the Wilderness   *Corliss Lamont*   5.95

____Rabbi and Minister   *Carl Hermann Voss*   7.95

## LIBRARY OF LIBERAL RELIGION

____Facing Death and Grief   *George N. Marshall*   7.95

____Living Religions of the World   *Carl Hermann Voss*   4.95

## PHILOSOPHY & ETHICS

____Animal Rights and Human Morality   *Bernard Rollin*   9.95

____Art of Deception   *Nicholas Capaldi*   6.95

____Beneficent Euthanasia   *M. Kohl, editor*   8.95

____Contemporary Analytic and Linguistic Philosophies   *E. D. Klemke*   11.95

____Esthetics Contemporary   *Richard Kostelanetz, editor*   11.95

____Ethics and the Search for Values   *L. Navia and E. Kelly, editors*   13.95

____Exuberance: A Philosophy of Happiness   *Paul Kurtz*   3.00

____Freedom, Anarchy, and the Law   *Richard Taylor*   8.95

____Freedom of Choice Affirmed   *Corliss Lamont*   4.95

____Fullness of Life   *Paul Kurtz*   5.95

____Having Love Affairs   *Richard Taylor*   8.95

____Humanhood: Essays in Biomedical Ethics   *Joseph Fletcher*   8.95

____Infanticide and the Value of Life   *Marvin Kohl, editor*   9.95

____Introductory Readings in the Philosophy of Science   *Klemke, Hollinger, Kline, editors*   12.95

____Invitation to Philosophy   *Capaldi, Kelly, Navia, editors*   13.95

____Journeys Through Philosophy (Revised)   *N. Capaldi & L. Navia, editors*   14.95

____Philosophy: An Introduction   *Antony Flew*                                            6.95

____Problem of God   *Peter A. Angeles*                                                    9.95

____Psychiatry and Ethics   *Rem B. Edwards, editor*                                       12.95

____Responsibilities to Future Generations   *Ernest Partridge, editor*                    9.95

____Reverse Discrimination   *Barry Gross, editor*                                         9.95

____Thinking Straight   *Antony Flew*                                                      5.95

____Thomas Szasz: Primary Values and Major Contentions   *Vatz & Weinberg, editors*        9.95

____Worlds of the Early Greek Philosophers   *Wilbur & Allen, editors*                     8.95

____Worlds of Hume and Kant   *Wilbur & Allen, editors*                                    7.95

____Worlds of Plato & Aristotle   *Wilbur & Allen, editors*                                7.95

## SEXOLOGY

____The Frontiers of Sex Research   *Vern Bullough, editor*                                8.95

____New Bill of Sexual Rights & Responsibilities   *Lester Kirkendall*                     6.95

____New Sexual Revolution   *Lester Kirkendall, editor*                                    6.95

____Philosophy & Sex   *Robert Baker & Fred Elliston, editors*                             8.95

____Sex Without Love: A Philosophical Exploration   *Russell Vannoy*                       8.95

## THE SKEPTIC'S BOOKSHELF

____Atheism: The Case Against God   *George H. Smith*                                      7.95

____Atheist Debater's Handbook   *B.C. Johnson*                                            10.95

____What About Gods? (for children)   *Chris Brockman*                                     4.95

____Classics of Free Thought   *Paul Blanshard, editor*                                    6.95

____Critiques of God   *Peter Angeles, editor*                                             9.95

## ADDITIONAL TITLES

____Age of Aging: A Reader in Social Gerontology   *Monk, editor*                          9.95

____Avant-Garde Tradition in Literature   *Richard Kostelanetz, editor*                    11.95

____Higher Education in American Society   *Altbach & Berdahl, editors*                    9.95

____Israel's Defense Line   *I.L. Kenen*                                                   9.95

____Pornography and Censorship   *Copp & Wendell, editors*                                 9.95


The books listed above can be obtained from your book dealer
or directly from Prometheus Books.
Please check off the appropriate books.
Remittance must accompany all orders from individuals.
Please include $1.50 postage and handling for first book,
.50 for each additional book ($4.00 maximum).
*(N.Y. State Residents add 7% sales tax)*

Send to _____
(Please type or print clearly)

Address _____

City _____ State_____ Zip_____

Amount Enclosed_____

**Prometheus Books**
**700 E. Amherst St.**
**Buffalo, New York 14215**